Francesc Eiximenis
An Anthology

Francesc Eiximenis
An Anthology

Introduction and selection of texts by
Xavier Renedo and David Guixeras

Translated by
Robert D. Hughes

BARCINO · TAMESIS
BARCELONA / WOODBRIDGE 2008

First published 2008
by Tamesis
in association with Editorial Barcino

ISBN 978 1 85566 162 2
COPYRIGHT DEPOSIT: B-3.873-08

Tamesis is an imprint of Boydell & Brewer Ltd
PO Box 9, Woodbridge, Suffolk IP12 3DF, UK
and of Boydell & Brewer Inc.
668 Mt Hope Avenue, Rochester, NY 14620, USA
www.boydellandbrewer.com

Editorial Barcino, S. A.
Acàcies 15. 08027 Barcelona, Spain
www.editorialbarcino.com

Designed and typeset by Jordi Casas

Printed in Spain by Grup 3

Cover illustration:
*Lluís Borrassà, Scene from the life of the Virgin Mary.
Detail from the reredos of the Presentation of the
Mother of God and Saint George, 1390.
Church of Saint Francis (Vilafranca del Penedès,
Catalonia).*

Contents

Introduction

JORGE LUIS BORGES USED TO SAY that the greatest virtue of anthologies lies in what they leave out. In an anthology of texts by Francesc Eiximenis, who wrote so much on so many subjects, omissions are bound to occur. For example, we have not included any of the author's prophetic texts, whose interest and influence are steadily gaining recognition, and there is little concerning the sin of gluttony and the art of good eating, one of the themes of Eiximenis' work best known by the general public. Neither have we produced an anthology of exempla, a genre in which Eiximenis' narrative art was at its best. Instead of a general anthology of his work, which would have had to include a multitude of themes in addition to those mentioned, we have narrowed our selection to a number of texts that set out our author's ideas on culture and education.

This book could be considered the result of a paradox – a paradox well explained by Evangelista Vilanova in his considerations on the origins of the Franciscan Order. "Francis and his friars, the 'poor of Christ', however disinclined they may have been to intellectual study in general, were a reforming force for theological studies in the schools and universities. They became teachers in those universities, leaving monastic traditionalism to its fate." In other words, an order which began life unconcerned with the world of books and intellectual study came to form an integral part of the mediaeval system of schools and universities, leading to the publication of an impressive number of studies on theological, philosophical and scientific subjects. Eiximenis' work is a good example of this, above all as a vehicle of communication in the vernacular for the culture of theological and university circles. He had first-hand knowledge of everything that was taught and written about in the universities of Europe, and shows his gift as a writer in works of the quality of *Lo crestià*, an encyclopaedia which although unfinished, consists of 2,592 chapters whose aim was no less than to communicate "briefly" to the inhabitants of the towns "all the essentials of Christianity."

The civilising rôle of the towns

Except for *Ars praedicandi populo*, a training manual for preachers, Eiximenis wrote no educational treatise in the strict sense of the term. However, his vast opus contains many reflections on educational questions. For reasons of space, we have not included all of these in our anthology, but have made a selection, dividing the texts into four chapters. The first of these covers Eiximenis' concept of wisdom, the methods for acquiring it, and the important rôle he considered to be played by the towns as centres for the spread of knowledge, and as the ideal setting for the religious and civil education of laymen.

As a good Franciscan, Eiximenis set a high value on prayer as a means of acquiring knowledge and wisdom through divine illumination. But this did not cause him to abandon traditional methods involving teachers in schools and preachers in church – methods that required a predominately urban setting. He had a clear idea of all aspects of the pedagogical and evangelical objectives of the new mendicant orders, whose aim, in the words of Carlo Delcorno, was the religious – and by extension civil – education of laymen. The best venue for this was clearly in the towns. A well-known Latin distich, almost proverbial in character, well explains this choice, and also the differences concerning this question that existed between the new mendicant orders and traditional monastic practice:

> *Bernardus valles, montes Benedictus amabat,*
> *oppida Franciscus, celebres Dominicus urbes.*[1]

This is an exact description of the situation, as the mendicant orders, above all the Franciscans and the Dominicans, built their convents in the very heart of the towns and were in daily contact with the inhabi-

---

[1] "Bernard loved the valleys; Benedict, the mountains; Francis, the towns, and Dominic, the famous cities".

tants, their problems and their needs. The towns in their turn bene-
fited from this. As Eiximenis tells us, they filled with "more learned
men, more books, more sermons, more lectures, and more examples
that are worthy from many fine people" (I, 3.5) and were the ideal
venue for full development of man's social and political potential. Eiximenis used a well-known Aristotelian definition to refer to man as "a
naturally social animal". The ideal Christian was he who lived in close
relationship with his fellows and for his fellows, reading books and
listening to sermons, seeking out teachers with whom to discuss the
questions that arose from his reading, and refining his language
through contact with the thousand different manners of speech to be
heard daily in the towns. There was no shadow of doubt that this ideal
was more likely to be achieved in an urban environment, and it was
therefore logical for Eiximenis to suggest to country-dwellers that if
they could afford the expense, it was best for them to send their sons
away to study in town. If the first sentence of Aristotle's *Metaphysics*
states that "All men have a natural desire to learn", the towns, for Eiximenis, constituted the ideal venue in which to satisfy this desire.

The chapters which deal with the age-old subject of *translatio studii*
(I, 4) – the history of the transmission of culture from its origins in the
East to the Europe of the towns and universities in which Eiximenis
lived and wrote his works – illustrate the degree to which he thought
culture was a thing predominantly of the towns. It is a question that
arises frequently in mediaeval chronicles and encyclopaedias, and
serves to show that science and learning had followed an uninterrupted, parallel path throughout history, and therefore, as Jacques
Verger has pointed out, came to be part of a providential plan. Eiximenis' presentation, as in other mediaeval authors, is also related to
translatio imperii – the continuing history of empire and political
power, which, like science and learning, had passed through a number
of different stages without interruption, always furthering the cause of
wisdom and learning. If *translatio studii* and *translatio imperii* often went
hand in hand, it was less common practice to associate these two
themes with praise of the rôle of the towns as centres for the spread of
science and culture from the beginning of human history – from the
period following man's expulsion from Paradise to the Europe of
mediaeval times. "Knowledge", writes Eiximenis, "arises from great
buildings and from towns and cities, and this is so by special order of
Our Lord God" (I, 4.8). Between Enos, the first town in history, and

Bologna, Paris, Oxford or Cambridge, the history of towns formed part of the same providential plan that controlled the transmission of knowledge and political power. This is the added value that Eiximenis brought to his original re-creation of an age-old medieval theme.

Education in the home

The second chapter of our book contains the principles which, according to Eiximenis, were to govern the education of children in the family home. As is to be expected, the father is the more important figure here, with the mother being allocated a secondary rôle. Indeed, the father was responsible for the education not only of his offspring, but also of the servants of the house and, given the great age difference that often existed between the spouses, that of his wife as well. For women, says Eiximenis, "it is quite natural [...] to be inclined to nurture children" (II, 1.2). A woman's rôle was limited to breast-feeding, providing nourishment and looking after the welfare of her younger children, but in principle she could not aspire to direct their moral and intellectual training as they grew up.

For Eiximenis, the father was the central figure in the family structure, and for him, therefore, lay the responsibility of his children's education and upbringing. His position as educator could not rely solely on severity or harsh treatment – children were to be educated through love. However, his authority over the servants, and at least part of their instruction, had to be carried out "with severity and fear, and not with love" (II, 1.1)[2]. The love involved in the education of children needed to be of a rational nature, and to be based on a regime of strict discipline that precluded excessively soft treatment, but without resorting to the use of violence. Eiximenis was extremely critical of those parents who "blinded by their love of their offspring, they do not take care to punish nor to reprimand their children" (II, 3.1), encouraging their bad habits and laughing at "all their follies and light-mindedness" (II, 2.3.1) To bring his message home, Eiximenis quotes dramatically clear proverbs from mediaeval tradition, or perhaps even of his own invention: "The man who does not raise his children well, invariably sounds his own death knell" (II, 2.3.1), or "he who rewards his sons too roundly deserves to be struck on the head

---

[2] Fear on the part of the servants also implied fear of being beaten by their masters: "Housemaids should be fearful of injury" (II, 5.3).

most soundly" (II, 2.3.2). In the chapters dealing with this subject, there are messages to be read between the lines which, albeit stated *en passant*, prove to be of great interest. According to Eiximenis, the tendency to spoil children was to be found more in mothers than in fathers, and was perhaps more common in widows than in women happily married. Eiximenis states this prejudice clearly in his *Llibre de les dones* (Book of Women), designed for a female readership, when he writes: "widows are wont to bring up their children badly, inasmuch as an ill-mannered child is usually known as a widow's nursling" (II, 2.3.3).

Corporal punishment was only to be resorted to when all else failed – when every teaching strategy had been tried to no effect. Here we have the delightful example of the sleepy Cambridge student (II, 4.2), a worthy campus companion for Rabelais' Gargantua. What was necessary was to find a point of balance between excessive severity and overtolerance – between the desperation of children, or students, made to suffer unbearable punishments the reasons for which they could not begin to comprehend, and the lack of discipline of the spoilt child who has been left without the guidance of God or man. Eiximenis has a range of advice to offer those who wish to find this point of balance. One suggestion is careful analysis of the desire to punish, in order to ascertain that the wish to correct really exists and that there is a real need for punishment, not just the initial reaction of anger that may manifest itself in a form difficult to recognise at first. Eiximenis also defends the principle of tolerance so as to avoid using a sledgehammer to crack a nut. On occasions punishment should be handled astutely, and seem to be mixed "with so much lard and so much honey and sweetness" (II, 3.5.3.), that at first sight it does not seem to be a punishment at all. What Eiximenis always recommends is that one should never lose one's composure or abandon good manners:

> the most gracious way there was of administering chastisement was if one were to let one's fury pass in such a way as to speak calmly, and then to take the criminal to task by explaining to him the seriousness of the crime he has committed and the penalty he deserves and what awaits him, and to say all this with a firm resolve and with measured rigour in one's sanction, yet without words of censure (II, 3.3).

Reason always had to guide the words and actions of the punisher, who had first to try all peaceful means at his disposal, and only resort to violent methods when there was no alternative. An extreme example of the subtle methods recommended by Eiximenis is the use of simulated anger, seemingly hard and unrelenting, yet in reality a fiction governed by the powers of reason.

The chapters dealing with the education of girls are of great interest. Eiximenis asks fathers – and husbands – to be understanding of the weaknesses of feminine nature, but then suggests they make strategic use – for the woman's own good – of the senses of fear and shame he says are characteristic of the sex. Eiximenis' inclusion of the husband here is due to the fact that women often married at a very early age, and it was left to the husband to complete the education that his young wife would have begun to receive from her parents. Fear and shame, as they appear in Eiximenis' works, are two basically passive states of mind that can be of great use for stunting development of the temptations and vices inherent in the weaker sex. The idea is often repeated: "Whoever raises a young girl should above all make her accustomed to feeling shame, for shame is the principal shield by means of which a girl must protect herself against evil. The next thing is that she should be fearful of her father and mother" (*LD* 18). To cultivate girls' sense of shame meant, for Eiximenis, encouraging them to keep silent and speak only when spoken to, not to play outside without permission from their mother, be modest in their looks and gestures, and keep their laughter at a discreet level. Cultivating this sense of shame in effect encouraged shyness in the girls and limited their spontaneity, at least in the outside world.

Cultivation of fear meant that parents had to be respected and obeyed, never allowing their daughters to answer back or argue. The threat of punishment was also to be made use of, initially at least, as a threat and no more. Eiximenis makes this clear: "have the stick at the ready for any misconduct, and wear a furious expression" (*LD* 18). But if the girl was stubborn and took no notice of the threats, then the moment had come for punishment to be applied; it was time to move from words to action.

Reading and writing in the late Middle Ages

Our third chapter contains what could be described as the programme of study and reading that Eiximenis proposed for the society of his time. It is a programme that emphasises the importance of learning and promotes the practice of reading and writing for all social classes – even for women and servants. The best illustration of the value Eiximenis gave to these practices occurs in a passage of the *Twelfth* book of *Lo crestià* (1385), where he speaks of the political – and therefore civil – obligation of parents to teach their children reading and writing. The younger generation could complain if their parents neglected this duty, thereby sentencing them to illiteracy, and denying them the possibility of escaping from "the darkness of ignorance":

> Alfarabius said *in suo Rudimentario* that sons have a right to lodge a civil complaint about the poor level of education they have received from their father if he has not, at the very least, taught them to read and write and to understand Latin as well, for without these things a man is as a fool among the people of the world (III, 5.2.2).

Although he never made any explicit statement to this effect, Eiximenis distinguished between at least two different levels in the teaching of writing, depending on the status of the students. For women, servants and members of the lower classes of society, it was sufficient to learn to read and write in the vernacular. The higher level, which also included the study of language and rhetoric, was reserved for princes, noblemen and well-to-do burghers. These two levels of the written language reflected the different responsibilities of the two groups of students – the one having the power to make decisions in political and economic life, while the other was relegated to domestic and secondary functions.

Eiximenis gives details of the plan of studies and reading matter designed for the prince, the nobles and the citizens or burghers. His ideas concerning the education of the prince can be summarised in a Latin aphorism, possibly by John of Salisbury – "*Rex illiteratus quasi asinus coronatus*" – translated by Eiximenis as "illiterate kings should not be called kings, but crowned asses" (I, 2.3.5). Another good illustration of his ideas is a short example concerning a character of the name of Geron, who, notwithstanding his illiteracy and advanced age, was made king of the unknown kingdom of Laxie, possibly an invention of Eiximenis'. So as to avoid becoming the "crowned ass" of the aphorism, he took on a crash course on literacy and reading:

> "I shall never reign or pass judgement until I am able to read."
> And within five months he was able to read, and he always read at night for the duration of two candles. And, consequently, nobody dared speak to him at night (III, 1.1).

The curriculum recommended by Eiximenis for the education of the prince is largely the same as that which he suggests for the sons of the nobility and the citizens. As all of these students were destined to hold political responsibility at court or in the cities, it was logical for them to share the same education and study the same subjects. Eiximenis recommends that both the prince's palace and the houses of the nobles and citizens should have a private study set aside for the practice of private reading and writing.

Study of the Bible logically had pride of place in these curricula, which were completed with study of other books on religious and moral subjects. Latin grammar had an important place in the *trivium*, as knowledge of this subject enabled students to read the books written in Latin that were good for their education, and made the use of interpreters unnecessary on diplomatic missions. After grammar, Eiximenis gives importance to the study of rhetoric, with a view to two significant activities in political and civil life – the art of giving good advice, and the skill of speaking in public. Eiximenis also defends the study of astrology and the basic principles of subjects such as arithmetic, geometry, natural philosophy, medicine and theology. For princes, he recommends study of the laws and charters of their kingdoms, of canon law, and – very important – the "histories and annals of their predecessors", which they had to know by heart. The sons of knights and nobles should make a detailed study of books concerning "the people, soldiery and political life" (III, 2.2). This meant the works of Giles of Rome, John of Wales, Vegetius or Valerius Maximus, which in the original Latin, or the many translations available in different vernacular languages, were to be found in the libraries of many princes and townsmen of mediaeval Europe.

Eiximenis was in favour of the education of the sons of noblemen, and deplored the decadence he perceived in this class of society, which had abandoned "the study of wisdom, which was their chief glory", to concentrate solely on the practice of arms. As a consequence of this, in Eiximenis' words, "today the sons of peasants throughout the world have taken command of the study of wisdom that the nobles have forsaken and they stand in judgement over these nobles and have taken their chief honours" (III, 3.2). Such comments were not uncommon in works by authors from the mendicant orders, close as they were to the social classes of the towns and the to-and-fro of urban life. Fifty years before Eiximenis' time, Robert Holcot, an English Dominican well known to our author, had written effectively the same: "Generally, the sons of the rich and powerful do not learn, while the sons of simple men rise to the highest positions in the Church thanks to their good character and learning." As Jacques Verger has pointed out in connection with France and England, the nobility did not often study at university, and students were mostly the sons of burghers from the towns. Many merchant or shopkeeper families rose to be part of the urban oligarchy when one of their sons graduated from university, above all if he had studied law. Eiximenis' complaints at the loss of influence on the part of the nobility must have arisen from this process.

Of note, especially in the context of the Crown of Aragon, is Eiximenis' increasingly strong defence of the education of women, advisable, he tells us, not only for religious reasons, but also from a practical point of view. Women who were able to read and write could stay at home reading books on religious or moral subjects, and could even take charge of the early stages of their children's education. They could also help in the business activities of their husbands, for example by taking sole charge of the correspondence when the merchants, the ideal citizen according to Eiximenis, were away from home. It is significant that Eiximenis is on the defensive in his initial support for the education of women, but later states his case much more strongly. In the *Third* book of *Lo crestià* (1384), he goes no further than to recommend that husbands should not prevent their wives from learning to read and write, but in the later books he clearly defends the right of women to literacy and to free themselves from "the darkness of ignorance".

Between school and university

In the fourth chapter we visit the classrooms of a mediaeval school and consider a variety of questions concerning the rôle of the teacher, the use of oral activities in the teaching system, and the daily routine considered ideal for study and learning. T.S. Eliot used to say that if you had problems understanding a poem, you should read it aloud. This idea fits in exactly with the practice in mediaeval schools and universities, in which the students' understanding of their texts depended wholly on oral guidance on the part of the teacher – his gestures and above all his oral commentaries, which often came to be annotated in the margin of the textbooks. In short, books were read more by the ears than the eyes, and in Eiximenis' view, better memorised for this very reason: "one is much better acquainted with what one has learnt by listening and as a result of a person's oral explanations than what one has read or studied by oneself" (IV, 3).

Some of Eiximenis' texts deal with another kind of reading that would have been part of his routine and that of many other intellectuals – reading in the solitude of a monastic cell. This silent reading was ideal for a technical treatise or a scholastic summa, or for quick consultation of an encyclopaedia or book of sermons. We can see examples of this kind of reading in several passages of Eiximenis' *Ars praedicandi populo*, in a fascinating chapter which sets out to teach mnemotechnical techniques to preachers, so that they could memorise the content of their sermons:

> Fifthly, you can use a book that you have been studying. You can picture to yourself such and such a sentence as being on such and such a page of the book in question, and another sentence as being on another page, and yet another in the right-hand column of the first page, and a different one in the left-hand column, or [you can visualise] a certain idea as having a paragraph mark at the beginning, or a different one as starting with a capital letter or bearing a cross or some other sign next to it, and so on.

The technique described in passages such as this one involves strictly visual and mental assimilation of the text. Eiximenis suggests memorising the most important contents by noting the position of the sentences on the page and the purely visual elements accompanying the words – a capital letter, crosses or other noticeable symbols, lines connecting paragraphs or different ideas. It is significant that Eiximenis prepared the layout of the autograph copy of his sermons with symbols and other details just as he describes in the *Ars praedicandi populo*, as this makes clear what kind of reading technique he had in mind for a right edition of his sermons.

Eiximenis also wrote a few pages describing the moral and professional profile of the ideal teacher. He had to be in full command of his subject matter and teaching technique. He had to know how to recognise the best gifts in his students and then develop these gifts, always maintaining formality and a critical attitude towards his charges so as not to hinder their progress. The students, on their part, had to treat the teacher with the utmost respect, but should not be afraid to express disagreement once they had listened carefully and had fully analysed his words: "it is permissible for him to ask him respectfully and to seek an answer" (IV, 1.3).

Our anthology ends with a number of texts on the daily routine that was considered correct for an intellectual – a routine whose most important aspects were moderation in eating habits, hours of rest and style of dress, in direct contradiction to the *modus vivendi* of the sleepy Cambridge student, but also avoiding the excesses of austerity to be seen in "certain inhuman men", who, says Eiximenis, opposed reasonable use of play in the process of education. This excess to a fault was also attributed to those intellectuals who, succumbing to the sin of curiosity, lost the sense of moderation in their reading and their studies, again just the opposite of the lazy Cambridge student. As a good Scholastic, Eiximenis defended play and honest pleasure both in and out of school – in class because it improved the efficiency of study and learning, and outside because it refreshed body and soul, acting as a tonic for the tension and fatigue caused by intellectual effort and emotional stress.

We hope that our anthology suffers from no omissions of a serious nature, and that our aim of giving a full overview of Eiximenis' ideas on education does not make for heavy reading. If this is so, the fault is ours and ours only. Eiximenis himself is in no way to blame.

Xavier Renedo

The life of Francesc Eiximenis

EIXIMENIS, AS HE HIMSELF MENTIONS in the introduction to the *First* book of his *Lo crestià*, was born in Gerona. We do not know the exact date of his birth, but Josep Perarnau situates it around 1330, as a Franciscan of the name of Francesc Eiximenis was ordained subdeacon at the church of Santa Maria in the village of Sants, near Barcelona, on 22 December, 1351. Eiximenis would have joined the order at an early age – "*a pueritia evocatus*", as is stated in the colophon to the *Pastorale*. We know that a sister of his was married in Gerona in 1380 to a notary of the name of Bernat Pintor, which indicates that Francesc came from a well-to-do burgher family.

Eiximenis' education, as was the custom among Franciscans, would have begun in the order's own schools, and was completed at the University of Toulouse, where he graduated as Master in Theology in 1374, having received political and financial support from the Crown. Before going to Toulouse, however, he studied the greater part of the advanced courses on offer at Oxford, which, to quote Albert G. Hauf, would certainly have constituted "the most significant part of his academic training". Robert Lerner has recently identified Eiximenis' "a very famous Doctor called Ulteredus, who was a black monk [i.e. a Benedictine]" as Uthred of Boldon, who "lectured on the Sentences" in Oxford "around 1354". In addition, Eiximenis may well have studied at the University of Paris, as a document published by Pep Vila in 2001 states that in 1364 our author received five golden florins as a grant for his proposed studies there. The source of this money was A. Francesc Camps, a collector of funds for religious purposes in the Diocesis of Gerona. Once in possession of his coveted degree, the result of so many years spent at the best universities of Europe, Eiximenis divided his time between teaching activities and literary creation. His first teaching posts were probably at Barcelona and Vic.

His first great literary project was *Lo crestià*, a vast introduction to the basic principles of Christianity intended to be in thirteen volumes, although he finally came to write only four. In May 1381, King Peter III was so interested in the *First* book of *Lo crestià* that he gave orders to the guard of the Franciscan convent in Barcelona to prevent Eiximenis from leaving the building until it was finished. Perhaps at that time Eiximenis was already being pressurised by the municipal magistrates of Valencia to take up residence in their city. In 1383 he had to go there as arbiter of Vidal de Vilanova's will, and he decided to stay permanently. He soon presented the magistrates with his *Regiment de la cosa pública* (Rule of the Commonweal), which he would eventually expand into the *Twelfth* book of *Lo crestià*, the volume of the encyclopaedia dealing with political questions. In 1384, Eiximenis declined the offer of becoming confessor to the Infante Joan, an office most other clerics would have rushed to accept. Clear proof of the interest of the Valencian City Council in Eiximenis' works is the fact that in that same year of 1384 any interested citizen could go to the Council Chamber and consult a copy of *First* and *Second* books of *Lo crestià* (the latter most likely finished in the city in 1383), and the *Regiment de la cosa pública*. The *Third* book of *Lo crestià*, written in 1384, was soon added, as were the two volumes of the *Twelfth*, which we know were finished by February 1387. In this way, all the parts of *Lo crestià* that Eiximenis came to finish were available for consultation in the Council Chamber.

But Eiximenis did more in Valencia than write his literary works. He was also an adviser and man of confidence for the city magistrates. Father Andreu Ivars has recorded twenty-two donations, the first occurring on 27 July, 1383, that were given to Eiximenis in recognition of his valuable advice and his work in the service of the community. Two examples of this work which are relevant to this anthology are the sermon the magistrates commissioned him to preach on the death of Peter III in 1387, and his participation in 1399 in the debate concerning municipal statutes that were established that year for the schools of the city.

After stopping work on *Lo crestià*, Eiximenis continued to publish. In 1392 he produced the *Llibre dels àngels* (Book of Angels), dedicated to Pere d'Artés, one of the most influential politicians of the Kingdom of Valencia. In 1396 he wrote the *Llibre de les dones*, dedicated to the Countess of Prades, and in 1403 came the *Vita Christi*, also dedicated to Pere d'Artés. Eiximenis was well-known in Valencia as a preacher, and it is unfortunate that none of his sermons has been preserved in its entirety. At least we have the *Ars praedicandi populo*, a manual designed to establish norms for the behaviour of preachers and the preparation of the content of their sermons.

Eiximenis enjoyed especially good relations with King Martin and his wife Maria de Luna. The king requested his advice on more than one occasion, and they often lent each other books. Eiximenis was with the king's wife at her deathbed, and was the executor of her will. Some years before, he had dedicated his *Scala Dei* to her – a devotional manual containing extracts from the *Llibre de les dones*.

In August, 1408, Benedict XIII –the Avignon Pope during this period of the Papal Schism– called Eiximenis to the Council at Perpignan, made him Bishop of Elne, and conferred on him the honorific title of Patriarch of Jerusalem. On 15 November 1408, he was ordained Bishop of Elne, but died in Perpignan a year later. In his will he left thirty-one of his books to the Franciscan monastery in Gerona, the school which would have been the starting-point of his education and of a career that was to make him one of the most widely read, most translated and most influential of the Catalan authors of the late Middle Ages and well into the 16th century.*

David Guixeras

---

* The Introduction and The life of Francesc Eiximenis are translated by Howard Croll.

Translator's preface

IN THEIR ORIGINAL CATALAN, the writings of Francesc Eiximenis reveal a very deliberate use of language and a consistency in terminology throughout, not to mention a characteristic reiteration of a broad though necessarily circumscribed range of issues. In translating this anthology, I have attempted to be faithful to the spirit of this 14th-century Franciscan if not to convey to the modern reader in an accessible manner the verve with which this author writes. To this end, I have taken the decision to introduce a certain degree of variation with regard to Eiximenis' often repetitive style. In so doing, I have used a selection of synonymous or near-synonymous terms and expressions in English to denote those key words used by this author with such rigour and regularity (e.g., *bon saber, ciència, correcció* and its cognates, *ira, vergonya/desvergonya, discreció/indiscreció* and cognates, *vituperi*, etc.). This is not to suggest, however, that Eiximenis is a severe and exclusively highbrow author, lacking in good humour; quite the opposite: this anthology is peppered with proverbs illustrating the popular wisdom of his time and with jokes and witticisms, all of which ultimately have, in the broadest possible sense, a moralistic or pedagogical purpose. In using a variety of means to translate such terms, I hope to have preserved these very purposes as well as the precise meanings which run throughout this anthology while rendering the texts themselves somewhat less ponderous to the modern reader. Often, in the case of Eiximenis' jokes, I have had to seek English equivalents for wordplay which, strictly speaking, resists immediate translation and, as regards his rhyming proverbs, to find solu-

tions that maintain a popular feel while subscribing to a more typi-
cally English sense of metre.

Another noteworthy characteristic of Eiximenis' style, and one frequent among medieval writers, is his recourse to quotation, mostly
Biblical but also from Classical sources. In the former case and in the
light of the fact that ultimately, at least, Eiximenis is a Catholic author
writing for a Catholic readership, I have been partially guided in my
translation of his own helpful translations or paraphrases of these quo-
tations by the Challoner revision (1749-1752) of the Douay-Rheims
Bible of 1609 (Tan Books and Publishers, Rockford, Ill., 1995 edition)
as well as by the Catholic edition of the Revised Standard Version of
the Holy Bible. Though the Douay-Rheims Bible is itself a translation
of the Latin Vulgate Bible translated by St. Jerome from the Hebrew
and Greek originals, I believe that I have not been led into infinite
regress by my recourse to this text, for precisely the reason that Eiximenis himself was referring to the text of the Vulgate, to which the
Douay-Rheims Bible (in its various forms) is the closest existing equivalent in the English language.

I should like to take the opportunity to thank my editor at Barcino,
Dr. Joan Santanach, for his continued professionalism, politeness and
good humour. My thanks also go to Montserrat Lluch Juncosa and
Francesc J. Gómez for the valuable insights they have provided into
the texts here presented and for their rigour as proofreaders.

Notes inserted by the translator are marked with an asterisk (*).

Robert D. Hughes
Prague and Sedlejovice, 2006-2007

Table of abbreviations of Eiximenis' works

DC   DOTZÈ DEL CRESTIÀ
(*Twelfth Book of the Christian Encyclopaedia*)

LA   LLIBRE DELS ÀNGELS
(*Book of Angels*)

LD   LLIBRE DE LES DONES
(*Book of Women*)

PC   PRIMER DEL CRESTIÀ
(*First Book of the Christian Encyclopaedia*)

RCP   REGIMENT DE LA COSA PÚBLICA
(*Rule of the Commonweal*)

SC   SEGON DEL CRESTIÀ
(*Second Book of the Christian Encyclopaedia*)

SD   SCALA DEI
(*Ladder of God*)

TC   TERÇ DEL CRESTIÀ
(*Third Book of the Christian Encyclopaedia*)

VC   VITA CHRISTI
(*Life of Jesus Christ*)

FROM PARADISE TO THE CITY

I

1. On human ignorance

1.1. *Original Sin and ignorance*

You must first note in this respect that original sin has left man with four great and terrible wounds, which are a natural source, principle and stimulus within him and lead him into every evil and sin. The first of these wounds is called ignorance; the second, covetousness; the third, wickedness; the fourth, powerlessness or infirmity or feebleness of nature. And of these Bede has spoken, and likewise the Master of the Sentences[1] in the Second Book, in the twenty-second Distinction, and various other Doctors have spoken about this at length. And Our Saviour alludes to these wounds – as we see in *Luke* X (29-37) in the figure of the man who travelled down from Jerusalem to Jericho – when He says that this person was robbed and wounded on the way and was later assisted by the Samaritan. For the Doctors say that, by this man, Our Saviour wished to refer to our father, Adam, who, not wishing to obey Our Lord God in his earthly paradise, nor the commandments that He issued to him, fell into the hands of robbers through his sin, that is to say, under the sway of devils and of various sins, by which sins he was robbed. For he lost the blessings of grace and was injured to his very core on account of the said four wounds, which he transmitted to us along with his original obligation and with many other hardships which we suffer every day in this present life.

TC 38

[1] *Master of the Sentences*: name by which Peter Lombard, author of the *Libri quattuor sententiarum*, was known.

1.2. A chapter which states that the first natural wound is ignorance, and which proves that it is a great affliction

The first of the said four wounds is called ignorance. And you should note in this respect the following points. For first be attentive and you shall see by experience how man is born ignorant of all things in this world, and unable to make his reason understand the things that he sees and hears or to inquire into any truth. And therefore Aristotle has stated in the first book of his *De anima* that when man starts out his soul is like a *tabula rasa* on which nothing has been painted or written.[2]

The second point is that theologians call this ignorance an affliction and a wound, and it is in us for the reasons designated above, whence springs man's original evil, namely Adam's first sin. And you may know why this ignorance is, with good cause, called an affliction, if you pay attention to the following reasons. The first is that you should think how deplorable it is in man that he should be a lofty and noble rational creature, yet that he be born as ignorant as a brute animal and that all that he learns he should have to know by dint of toil and trouble. And of this did David complain when he said *Homo cum in honore esset non intellexit. Comparatus est iumentis insipientibus, et similis factus est illis* (Ps 48,13). And he meant that it was a great shame that man, whom God had created in such honour, nobility and wisdom, should have so withered in his descendents and the succession of his sons that by his ignorance he be compared and likened to senseless and rude animals, such as donkeys or billy- and nanny-goats and the like, and should be similar to one of them. [...]

Consider, fourthly, how great a shame is the following, namely that Our Lord God should have created as noble and excellent a creature as is the entire world in the service of man, as appears in *Genesis, capitulo* I (29-31), and that man should not appreciate what his own beauty and nobility is, nor how very keenly and subtly he is knit together and assembled, nor the profound wisdom with which he is ruled, governed and preserved, nor the arrangement or locations of heavenly bodies, nor their noble influence and beauty, nor the composition and order of the elements, nor the species, kinds and capacities of birds, fish and animals, and of other riches that the world possesses. In truth, he who considers this must feel great sorrow that, through his ignorance, he has forfeited contemplation, accurate study and clear knowledge of

[2] Cf. *De anima* III, 4.

these such lofty things, and that he should stand amidst all these wonders just like a donkey in a stable. Fortunatus said the following, therefore, speaking of the state of wretchedness in which our souls find
themselves in this world:

"Oh my dear soul! How can you be so blind and dumb amidst the
so many wonders that your Creator has given you and placed before
you? Oh you wretch! Pray to Him with all your strength night and day
that, since He has placed such a beautiful mirror before you, He might
wish to heal you of your blind ignorance so that, by contemplating
such lovely things, you might be aroused and stirred ever to love and
to praise Him."

TC 39

1.3. *How some types of ignorance are culpable and others deserving of sympathy*

You must note in this respect that certain kinds of ignorance are culpable and sinful and others not. Culpable ignorance is what occurs when
someone is wilfully unaware of that which he is obliged to know for the
sake of his salvation, such as the chief Articles of Faith, as is stated in the
Fifth book regarding matters of faith, and the general commandments
of the Holy Church, such as those concerning confession and receiving
Communion and Holidays of Obligation and similar things. And these
are thus things which it is necessary to know and from which man is not
excused by his ignorance while he is of an age to know them, except for
when that person is in a place where there is not or cannot be a teacher
regarding the aforesaid things: in that case an indomitable kind of ignorance would excuse him towards God.

TC 41

2. PATHS TO WISDOM

2.1. *Remedies for purging oneself of the said ignorance*

Let him who wishes to purge himself of this very great affliction of
ignorance pay attention to the remedies stated in this respect by my
lord Saint Augustine in his book, *De doctrina christiana,*[3] and in various
other places, for they are as follows. The first is devout prayer, for he

---

3 *De doctrina christiana* IV, 15 and 30.

states that this reveals important things. The second is to have a great desire for true wisdom. The third, to listen willingly, reverently and gladly to anyone who speaks the truth, whether he be great or lowly or whoever he may be. The fourth, that one should lead an orderly life in matters of eating and drinking and in all that one does. The fifth is gladly to read and often. The sixth, to not be ashamed of asking about things regarding which you have doubts, yet always to do so with humility and without presumption. The seventh, that what you know, you should willingly teach to others, without the slightest hindrance. The eighth, that you should not pursue carnal delights nor learn in order to make progress in material affairs, but rather so as to know Who God is and to do His will. The ninth, that you should continue any worthy endeavour that you begin. The tenth, that when you have learnt something new, you should immediately give thanks to Our Lord God.

Severus gives the following advice to those who really wish to learn to rid themselves of all ignorance, that is to say: to live chastely; to not be presumptuous, but always to ask and to learn with humility; to discuss or speak often about that which you wish to know; to consider devoutly those things you doubt and, subsequently, to offer a prayer to God and to the angel that watches over you; and to pay attention and be diligent in matters of learning. I have spoken at length on this subject at the beginning of the first book of the first part of the *Summa philosophica*, where I have dealt with metaphysical truth [...] and I have done this so as to give guidance to students and to those who are earnest in their search for knowledge and their flight from ignorance.

For the moment, what little we have said here on the subject is sufficient for laymen, to whom attending to erudite study is of no great concern. Note in this respect, however, that although more good and holy men have been ignorant and simple than great scholars and learned men, this, however, has been the great fault of those who are learned, for the gift of knowledge is a great gift from God and strongly disposes men to perform great offices for His love, honour and glory when the person who possesses the said knowledge is a man of good conscience and fears and loves God. And such a man is a great pillar of the Christian Church and worthy of a dual honour, according to what the Apostle has said, in writing *Ad Timotheum* (2 Tim 3,14-17), and Saint Jerome teaches this also in the many examples he gives in the prologue he wrote about the entire *Bible*. However, those who, through their love of Jesus Christ, have wished to renounce all learning and have utterly devoted themselves to a true and thoroughgoing service of God, are raised higher, just like the holy apostles and martyrs, and like Saints Benedict and Francis. For Our Lord God, who saw their righteous, pure and full resolve with regard to Him, and realised that they wished for but Him alone, gave Himself to them entirely, and was for them their perfect love, their sublime knowledge, their complete virtue and renown, their glorious repute, their recreation in their labours, and the purpose and continual delight of their hopes. The ignorance of these men was a ladder by means of which to ascend to true knowledge, and it was the key offering access to God's treasures. For this reason, I pray that you love and pursue this ignorance, if God grants that you should desire it, or, at least, that you honour it in those in whom it resides, so that they who have attained it might give succour to your weakness and might obtain mercy for you from their beloved friend and father, Jesus Christ.

TC 55

2.2. *Four paths to wisdom according to Hugh of Saint Victor*

2.2.1. *Which states that the sixth way in which cities can help one to be self-sufficient, consists of knowledge, learning and wisdom*

The sixth way that cities and communities can help one to become self-sufficient consists of knowledge, learning and wisdom. And, as Saint Jerome has stated, there is as great a distance between a learned and an ignorant man as there is between light and dark and, therefore, any man of worth must do all he can to acquire learning, and that learning should be commendable and should help him achieve the principal purpose for which both man and cities are made, that is to say, so as to govern themselves well and virtuously in order that they might have the kingdom of God. And Saint Jerome says that such learning is true philosophy and true Christian knowledge, and therefore Prosper concludes *in epistula sua Ad Bavarum* that every good citizen[4] is a noble philosopher, for, as he states in this very letter, a philosopher is nothing other than a man who lives virtuously. And as

---

4 In its primary sense of 'an inhabitant of a city or town'. I have consistently translated the Cat. *ciutadà* as 'citizen' in this sense, where other translators might have preferred something such as 'townsman', as I feel that this latter term does not cover all the contexts in which Eiximenis uses this word.*

Saint Augustine says, in the eighth book of his *De civitate Dei, capitulo primo,* since the true meaning of the word 'philosophy' should be love of virtue and of wisdom, it follows that every good citizen loves virtue and wisdom and, consequently, can be called a noble philosopher.

DC 185

2.2.2. How men are led to true wisdom through diligently seeking it and avoiding that which impedes it

Secondly, the other route which leads the good citizen to true wisdom and makes him a great philosopher is to seek it with great diligence. We read, therefore, in the second chapter of *Proverbs: Si quaesieris eam quasi peccuniam et quasi thesauros efoderis illam, tunc intelliges et invenies eam* (2,4-5). And this means that, if you wish to attain this lofty wisdom and philosophy and desire to seek it, do not idly devote yourself to it but do so most intently. And he gives the following example of this, by telling us to observe how diligently, attentively and studiously the person who searches for money and who digs the earth to find treasure, seeks that for which he is looking; thus, if you were to seek to discover with such diligence what true wisdom is, and where it resides and how it can be found, without any doubt, God would give it to you eventually.

Commenting upon this versicle, Chrysostomus says the following in one of his homilies: Do you wish to find wisdom? Know that you must have it from God. Do you wish Him to give it to you? He desires that you should ask Him for it with eagerness, and that you should labour tirelessly for it. And thus, without any doubt, you can expect to have it, for Saint James has said that if someone desires wisdom, let him ask God for it (Jas 1,5), Who is its source and origin, and let him ask for it most insistently, that is to say, by continually doing as much as he can for, without any doubt, he will obtain it, since He who cannot lie has said, when teaching us how to acquire it: "Ask, and if you persist, you shall have what you desire, for to him who persists will the door finally be opened" (Mt 7,7-8 and Lk 11, 9-10). And, if you wish to know, said Aimo in one of his sermons, how to obtain heavenly wisdom to the degree of which we are capable; then, certainly, it is by praying to Him from whom it must derive, and by continual study of that wisdom, while disdaining all work, and by going in search of many good books and by seeking worthy educators and teachers.

The third route which leads man to true philosophy and true wisdom is to avoid all things which might prevent him from attaining it, for the devil, when he sees that someone wishes to be a wise and true philosopher, immediately places obstacles along the route, while watching to see how first he might hinder him. And Saint Gregory states this in his *Morals* when he says that the devil carefully observes those who wish to be worthy and considers those vices towards which they are inclined, and if he sees that they are inclined towards avarice, he says the following to them:

"Why do you not amass wealth so as to become a great and rich man instead of going in pursuit of mad ideas? What is all the learning in the world worth if a man is without honour, rank and riches from which he might live?"

And it is in this way that, if the devil were able forever to bind man up in a love of wealth, from then on such a man would not devote himself to being either wise or worthy. The reason for this is that avarice and the love of riches make man so wicked and riddled with every evil that they do not allow him to be worthy nor to know what is commendable nor to come close to anything which might be so.

Holy Scripture states, therefore, in *Ecclesiasticus* X, that *Nichil nequius quam amare peccunias* (10,10). And it means that there exists nothing in the world which prevents man from attaining God or His wisdom as much as the love of money and riches, for such a man considers all time that is not spent amassing a fortune as being to no avail, and all the money that he devotes to good books as being ill-spent – it is sufficient for him, if he has to read a little, that he should have books which are borrowed – and all the money that he gives to worthy teachers he bemoans and considers to be wasted. So, how could such a man ever be wise or worthy? In truth, it is an impossible thing. Therefore, we read that the first thing done by the great philosophers who wished to turn their thoughts to wisdom, was either to renounce their wealth or, if they retained it, they ceased to amass any more, but instead took advantage of their riches in order to acquire wisdom and to be great philosophers.

The eminent philosopher Socrates used to say that carnal desires did not prevent man from acquiring wisdom as forcefully as did the rapacious desire to amass a fortune, and he proved this in the following way: for, he said, carnal appetites do not assail man at all times, but rather can man soothe them by many means and, later, they cease in old age, but greed is so firmly rooted in the heart that it never leaves man, but rather, as he grows older, so does his greed increase.

DC 187

2.2.3. *Which sets out those things that rapidly bring wisdom to man*

When the great philosopher Plato was asked which things helped men to become wise in a short space of time, he cited the following reasons in his reply: the first was to seek a peaceful location and to avoid all other tasks; the second, humbly to listen to everybody who might teach them; the third, being in a foreign land; the fourth, to maintain poverty and not to have an excess of anything; the fifth was to have conversations with learned people; and the sixth, to concentrate upon it, for concentration makes man a master.[5]

The versifier said that *gutta cavat lapidem non vi, sed saepe cadendo,* and he meant that the drop erodes the stone little by little, rather than all at once; in this way, the wise man exercises great diligence in learning little by little, rather than all at once. Saint Jerome mentions, in the first chapter of the prologue that he wrote about the *Bible,* the great diligence and sustained effort that various philosophers had to learn, by which diligence they arrived at great wisdom and excellence in their moral life, for all learning should end in living a good life since to live well is its aim. Saint Augustine, therefore, states, in his *De civitate Dei,*[6] that the great philosopher Socrates directed all his philosophical erudition towards knowing how to live well in every respect and to correct his vices and to live virtuously. And, therefore, Saint Augustine said, *decimo nono De civitate Dei,* capitulo I, that a philosopher should never chiefly learn nor labour for anything other than to live a good life and ultimately to attain happiness in God.

DC 188

2.2.4. *How appreciating and honouring wisdom makes it possible for man to obtain it*

The said Doctor has stated that the fourth way to attain wisdom is to appreciate and to honour it, and to make good use of it after it has

---

5 Cf. Hugh of Saint Victor, *Didascalicon* III, 12. The author of this list was, in fact, Bernard of Chartres.

6 Cf. *De civitate* Dei VIII, 3.

been attained, for without these things it cannot remain in man and to attain it by another means is not to attain it, but to put it out of one's reach. For there are certain people, according to what Saint Ambrose has said in a sermon, who ultimately attain wisdom and a virtuous life, but for whom the sound use of their fine wisdom does not last long. And these men are accursed by God and are as swine who have before them pearls and precious stones and know not how to do anything with them but to thrust them into the mud with their snouts; and so, these men, often through the pride that they feel on account of their learning and their worthy living, fall into the devil's mire, that is to say, into pride and vainglory. And by such means, they succumb to other great sins and, just as they should be a light for others, so they are the cause of their yielding to evils similar to those into which they have fallen. Jesus Christ spoke against such men, in *Luke* XI, saying: "Woe unto you, learned men of the law who have taken away the key to God's wisdom; you never wished to enter directly, but rather forbade this to those who were entering" (11,52).

Seneca, *in quadam epistola*, says that the greatest possible abuse there is, is to misuse the best tools that God has provided for the purpose of attaining happiness. These tools are philosophising and possessing wisdom and being able to live a good life, and if man has all these things yet abandons them for the sake of anything else, he offers a sufficient indication that he has readily chosen death and eagerly desires to be mad and to be esteemed among brute animals. Oh!, said Chrysostomus in this respect, and what will Christians do under the great and severe judgement of God, if philosophers, in order to live virtuously, should abandon their lands, their relations, their riches and all their pleasures, and should seek to discover throughout the entire world how they might correct their vices and liberate themselves from all evil and live according to the judgements of right reason? Certainly, these men will bring shame upon us all, for these people without a law have performed works of the law, and we who possess a law have with our ill deeds impugned the law of God. And Policraticus, *libro tercio, capitulo nono,*[7] said the following: "Dear God!, for who in Christendom has seen greater chastity than that shown by Socrates, nor greater loyalty than that shown by Fabricius, nor better judgement than that of Fronto, nor greater diligence in his affairs than that of Themistocles,

7 John of Salisbury, *Policraticus* III, 9.

nor greater purity than that of Scipio, nor greater patience than that
of Ulysses, nor such abstinence as that of Cato, nor such piety as that
of Titus?" Certainly, the whole world must marvel at these men who,
since they did not have great knowledge of God nor were their virtues
in fact virtues, but only images and similitudes of virtues, insofar as
they were not founded upon true faith nor upon true charity, according to what Saint Augustine says in *De civitate Dei*,[8] nevertheless showed
us, who await the kingdom of God as our reward, a great example of
how to live virtuously, for they performed so many and such great wonders in the way that they lived, though never expected any other
reward beyond the present world.

DC 189

2.3. *Five paths to wisdom according to Origen*

2.3.1. *How sovereigns should first do everything in their power to ensure that they enjoy good judgement and wisdom*

Among all the virtues necessary to any regent is wisdom, according to
what is stated by Holy Scripture and to the dictates of reason. Therefore the great Hermes Trismegistus said, when writing to the Roman
Senate, *Addiscite et audite sapientiam qui iudicatis terram*. And since he was
speaking to the regents of this world, he meant the following: Learn
and listen to wisdom, you who judge the peoples of this earth. And
David said the following in his *Psalm: Exaudimini, qui iudicatis terram* (Ps
2,10). And he, similarly, meant this: Oh you, who judge this earth, educate yourselves and do all you can to be wise! And that great Doctor,
Origen, states that the man who wishes to attain and to enjoy wisdom
by human arts and means must acquire it in five ways: the first, through
special prayers and supplication to Our Lord God; the second, through
private study and contemplation; the third, through instruction from
teachers or companions; the fourth, through accurate analysis;[9] the
fifth, through continuous experience and transaction.

Solomon had it in the first way, which is by special prayers, according to what we read in the third book of Kings (3,6-9), for, when he
was a child and incapable of governing the people of God, he
implored Our Lord God to give him the good sense and wisdom by

8 Cf. *De civitate Dei* V, 18.
9 Cat. *per literal declaració*: scholastic hermeneutical method conducted at the literal
(or historical) level.*

which he might rule his people, and Our Lord God gave it to him in abundance. Philo,[10] therefore, said with regard to himself, *Sapientiae septimo: Invocavi et venit in me spiritus sapientiae* (7,7). And he means that he implored Our Lord God to make him wise, and that then the spirit of wisdom came upon him, for Our Lord God is accustomed to giving his gifts to those who ask for them confidently and by continuous entreaty and who prepare themselves for it by improving their lives. Saint James, therefore, said the following in his *Epistle*, namely *Si quis indiget sapientia, postulet in fide a Deo, qui dat affluenter et non improperat* (Jas 1,5). And he means this, namely that if anyone lacks wisdom, let him ask God for it, and let his petition be made with great confidence, for Our Lord God gives generously of it to the person who prepares himself worthily to receive it, and when He has given it He does not throw reproaches in one's face, as do the people of this world, but rather He is prepared to give more and more of it, if that person who requests it knows how to ask for it correctly.

DC 496

2.3.2. Which states the second way in which one can have wisdom, and why a person who is mad should on no account be placed in the position of ruler

The second way of acquiring wisdom for oneself is by private study and contemplation, as David has written in his *Psalm*, namely *Signatum est super nos lumen vultus tui, Domine* (Ps 4,7). And, addressing God, he means the following: You have placed upon us, Lord, the sign of Your countenance, that is to say, You have placed natural intelligence within us, by which we are made similar to You, for You are all reason, good sense and wisdom, and by which we are capable of knowing what is evil and what is good and of seeing keenly how the things we are supposed to do should be done and how not. It is very true, as Aristotle states in his *Politics*, that from wherever the use of natural intelligence proceeds, this said intelligence and good sense is, nevertheless, not in all men equally, for some have intelligence to a very high degree, others moderately and others to such a low degree that they appear to be brute animals rather than men. And whoever's good sense and intelligence is as low as this latter degree, should under no circumstances enjoy the position of lord or ruler, for it would serve

---

[10] *Philo*: the name of a learned Jew to whom some Fathers and Doctors of the Church attributed authorship of the Biblical Book of *Wisdom*.

just as well to place an animal there and to sow discord across all his territories, as it would to give that position to someone with such little
sense. And whoever consents to the rule of such a man will ultimately
be dashed to pieces by divine judgement, for the first person to whom
he will deal a blow shall be the one who consented against his conscience to that man's becoming ruler; and God has shown many examples of this in various parts of the world.

And, according to what is stated by Saint Augustine, since the merits of the many good people who are in the community enable their
protests against any villainous man who overthrows it to ascend to God,
if a person exerts himself more on behalf of a madman alone than on
behalf of the entire community, and does not hesitate to allow the community to be brought down in order to raise a madman on high, it is
quite reasonable that this person should feel the knife of God fall upon
him and upon his family as a result of such protests. The great philosopher Leucippus, therefore, said that to place lordship into the hands of
a mad person was to place a knife in the hands of a violent man. And
when Anaxagoras, the celebrated philosopher, was asked what a mad
sovereign was, he replied that he was a crowned ass, for he said that the
madman and the ass were brothers and the particular sons of madness
and poor sense. Madness was their mother and Poor Sense their father,
and their sons were called Mules and Billy-goats, and their daughters
Cowardice, Lack of Concern and Scant Virtue. The great philosopher
Zeno said, therefore, that when a sovereign is mad, it is a sign that his
subjects are billy-goats and mules, and that they are filled with cowardice and lack of concern, and have little good in them or virtue, and
that they are better suited to being slaves than to having liberty and
freedom.

DC 497

2.3.3. *How a sovereign can acquire wisdom for himself by private study and
thought, which is the second way*

Nevertheless, those who are moderately intelligent and have moderately good sense can be placed in positions of governance, and much
more so those who have these qualities to a supreme degree, for, as
Aristotle says *in secundo Politicorum*, the more sense and intelligence a
man has, the better is he suited to governing others. This is because it
befits such men to ponder and to study by themselves when they are

resting from their affairs, for as we find *in septimo Physicorum: Anima sedendo et quiescendo fit prudens*,[11] and it means that the soul becomes wise when man is at rest, for then is the time to think, when nothing external can disturb one's mind.

And at these times, in order to rule his people well, the good regent must think about the following things, which will make him wise if he gladly puts them into practice, as Polycarp has written in his *Commentaries*. The first is this: How does he stand in relation to God? That is to say, does he show marked ingratitude to Him for His great benificence and is he highly negligent in fighting on behalf of His honour and glory in all of his deeds? The second is this: Considered in himself, what does he think are his failings as a sovereign? If he is overly impulsive or overly confident in his rule, let him correct this immediately. In particular, let him pay heed to whether he causes himself to be the object of scorn, that is to say, in his bearing or in his manners, for a sovereign must offer an example to others in all his gestures in order that his rule be not despised by others. The third is that he should begin to consider how he performs his office and how he behaves towards his people, that is to say, whether he ensures that they have true, speedy and transparent justice, free from corruption; whether he has bad officials; whether the common people are heard; whether villainous people are eradicated; whether the worthy are treated with respect, and whether there are protests from any part. And he should attend to every man without delay, to the best of his ability and in the manner which seems most appropriate to him. The fourth is that he should ask himself how he behaves towards his servants and officials, and which ones should be replaced and which retained; and, by asking the people, he should secretly inquire how these officials govern and whether they commit offences against anyone. The fifth is that he should consider how he stands with regard to foreign countries, both friend and foe, near and far; and he should think about how he might get along better with all of them, by keeping peace in mind at all times rather than honour, unless there should be some significant loss of prestige, for in such a case this loss of prestige would cause the peace to crumble in an instant.

DC 498

---

[11] Cf. *Physics* VII, 3.

2.3.4. How man can acquire wisdom from instruction, and this is the third way

The third human way of acquiring wisdom for oneself is from instruction by teachers or companions. And primarily from teachers, for, according to what the great Plutarch states in his *Elementaries*, every sovereign must have at his side the best possible man that he can find, of whatever estate he might be, who should be learned, conscientious, virtuous and true, and at least such that he be less wicked than other men. And this man should never separate himself from the sovereign, but rather should assist him by his guidance in bearing the burden of his rule and should conceal his failings. And this is what the great sovereigns used to do in olden times, for, according to what Aulus Gellius states, *Atticarum noctium*, Alexander the Great always had the great philosopher Aristotle as his teacher; and the Roman emperor, Tiberius Claudius, had Seneca; and the emperor Trajan had Plutarch; and Julius Caesar had Leontius; Caesar Augustus, Clancolus; Constantine, Almaxui; Charlemagne, Alcuin; Theodorus, the holy Abbot Evandrus, and so on for many others. And these teachers were under orders to tell them all their failings in private and they taught them all those things which could help a person to live a good life and to govern his subjects admirably, and they taught them a number of the sciences, as a result of which everyone feared to speak in front of sovereigns with regard to any matter, since they assumed that they were very knowledgeable on every matter.

It also helps one a great deal to acquire wisdom if one receives instruction from one's companions, that is to say, if one consorts with worthy people, for sovereigns listen more gladly to those who share their company than to those who are their teachers insofar as, by the corruption of our nature, we do not much care for those who have the task of educating us and we prefer those who accompany us through good times and bad. And if these people are able to speak skilfully, they can be of great benefit to a sovereign. Therefore sovereigns must always have wise men rather than knaves as their companions, for as the popular saying goes: a person is judged by the company he keeps. And therefore the proverb says, "Tell me about those with whom you can be found and I shall tell you whither your deeds are bound." For this reason, sovereigns who wish to be wise should be served by and keep company with wise men and then, withoubt doubt, they shall become very wise.

When Philetus, king of Syria, was asked why he committed so many follies while at home, considering that he was a wise young man and knew how to behave very sagely outside with respect to his subjects, he replied as follows:

"When I was young, my companions accustomed me so much to acting foolishly while at home that now I am almost unable to refrain from carrying on like this, but, if you were to change the company I keep, I would turn such folly into good."

And they did this, and once he began to associate with worthy and sensible young people, he became very wise and very tempered and a noble sovereign.

DC 499

2.3.5. *How man can acquire wisdom by extensive learning and heavy reading, and this is the fourth way*

The fourth way is through accurate analysis, that is to say, that he should learn to read well and should study worthy books, and such as give him instruction on how to lead a good life and how to be able to govern well. Writing to the emperor Theodosius, Saint Ambrose asked how sovereigns could possess and read useless books when they did not have time for the essential ones, however wisely they spent it. No man in this world requires more time than a good sovereign and none wastes more than a bad one, for such a man devotes all his time to follies and to the greatest damnation of his soul when, however, no one needs to concern himself with better things and greater learning more than a sovereign, since the strength of his knowledge constitutes the life of his subjects, according to what Policraticus has said, *libro quarto.*[12] According to what Boethius asserts, *libro primo De consolatione, capitulo quarto,* Plato therefore says that the commonwealth, in that case, would achieve its perfection in all that was good if it were governed sagely by a man who was conversant with the study of wisdom. Vegetius Renatus said, therefore, that the work of kings was to be learned, to govern and to judge. The emperor Foca wrote to the king of France that he should always devote himself to true knowledge, for illiterate kings should not be called kings, but crowned asses. Also we read in *Ecclesiasticus* X that *Iudex sapiens iudicabit populum suum, sed rex insipiens deperdet illum* (10,1-3). And it means that a learned and expert

---

[12] Cf. John of Salisbury, *Policraticus* IV, 4.

judge is suited to governing his people, but a foolish king lacking any worthwhile knowledge will have undermined them and lost them in no time at all.

Suetonius, in his book *The Twelve Caesars*, said that the most potent means there is in the world of causing a great sovereignty to topple was if the sovereign were a man without any profitable knowledge or afflicted by great madness. And in order to teach this truth to the entire world, Our Lord God wishes the famous and distinguished rulers of his beloved people to be wise and well-informed men. And it is clearly thus, for Abraham, who was the leader of and father to God's people, received thorough instruction in all forms of knowledge and wisdom associated with the great school of Egypt, and Moses was a great astrologer, according to what is stated by the Master of Histories,[13] and it is clear that David, as we read *secundo Regum* XIV, was an angel in his wisdom (2 Sam, 14-17), *et in primo Regum* we find that he behaved very wisely in all matters, and Solomon, and others after him (3 Kings 4,29-34).

DC 500

3. TEACHERS, BOOKS AND SERMONS

3.1. Which sets out the second main reason why cities were built, namely in order to avoid ignorance

The second main reason why our forefathers built cities and why they said that they should be built was in order to avoid ignorance and to know everything which is profitable and necessary to man with respect to his body and soul. For this reason, you must know in this respect that among the great scourges of this world that our first father, Adam, brought upon us, the foremost was ignorance, according to what the Master of the Sentences states in the second book, *distinctione* XXII. And this scourge was so great that, according to what Aristotle says *in primo De anima*, when we are born our souls are thus like a *tabula rasa* on which nothing is painted,[14] for, at that time, we know nothing, understand nothing, recollect nothing and reason not at all, on

---

[13] *Master of Histories*: the name by which Peter Comestor, author of the *Historia scholastica*, was customarily known.
[14] See above, note 2.

account of which we incur many faults and, later, very great afflictions and ills.

Because of this, it says in *Jeremiah, capitulo* X: *Stultus factus est omnis homo a scientia sua* (10,14), or, in other words, everybody is as good as a fool through lack of true wisdom for, even though all our wisdom should be brought to bear principally upon knowing God and our own conscience, we nevertheless do not know what God is, and once we are in a position to know this we do not wish to know it, corrupted as we are by natural ignorance; because of this, we are at all times worthless and devoid of all goodness. We read the following, therefore, *Sapientiae* XIII: *Vani sunt omnes homines in quibus non est scientia Dei* (13,1), and it means that all men are wretched and worthless who do not possess knowledge of God, namely who do not wish to understand, learn or know what God is. For knowledge and consideration of what God is immediately sets men to thinking about a great wonder, and this wonder puts them in fear, and this fear induces and inclines their hearts to honour and love that Lord whom they know to be so lofty, so worthy and so great. Therefore He has commanded us, through the psalmist, in these words: *Vacate et videte quoniam ego sum Deus* (45,11), and, in addressing us, He means this: Bear in mind, consider and realise that I am your God, for, if you do this, you shall praise and love Me just like good sons.

Saint Augustine said that nobody can love what he does not know;[15] so, if we wish to love God, we must have knowledge and understanding of Him, for in that case we shall recognise our wretchedness and humble ourselves, whether we wish to or not, before his lofty majesty. [...]

DC 10

3.2. *Which teaches the number of ways man is better able to free himself from his natural ignorance in notable and populous towns than he is in solitude*

In order, therefore, to avoid this ignorance so beset with perils, Our Lord God has made provision by greatly inclining men to build notable cities and communities, and He has done this so that in these places they might more suitably be able to inform themselves with regard to learning and wisdom in the following ways:

---

[15] Eiximenis seems to be referring to *De civitate Dei* XIV, 14.

First, by receiving instruction from teachers, for in these places a single teacher is sufficient to educate ten thousand other people about such things all of a piece, which instruction cannot take place in solitude.

And second, by example of experience, for in sizeable communities everybody can see what the others are doing, what they are saying and how they live, and thus do they learn.

And third, from the teaching of brothers or fathers, for, as there are many people there, in such places everyone can instruct his fellow man in what he needs to know as he would his brother, and a man can inquire much more conveniently there about everything, in general, that must be done, than he can in solitude.

And fourth, by private study, for, although a man who is isolated and in a state of solitude has more opportunity to read than he who lives in a village or town, he does not have, however, greater opportunity to learn, for the man who learns does not only require the opportunity to read, but also to ask how what he reads is to be understood. And learning is precisely a question of this, for, as the common saying goes, *legere et non intelligere negligere est,* which means that to read in order to study and yet not to understand is nothing short of a waste of time, because whoever wishes to study by reading must have a teacher close to hand, which teacher one is unable to find so easily in solitude as in society, unless one says that God makes up for every lack when one is alone. But this does not happen all the time nor with every type of person, since God's teachings with respect to man are supernatural and He wishes men not to tempt Him by expecting nothing other than to hear these teachings whenever they wish to find out about anything, but rather He wishes them to do what they are capable of doing and then He will make up for the remaining deficit through His great goodness, as He pleases. The holy abbot Theodorus recommended, therefore, that it is better for the man who wishes to learn about lofty, holy matters to spend a limited time among the perils which exist in cities than to flee them for lonely places and there to live without instruction and schooling. And he said that to live in solitude does not fall to the lot of anyone more than to him who knows and feels what perils there are and who has already been tested by various temptations, all of which things have first to be done among communities and settlements before man enters into solitude. [...]

DC 11

3.3. *That teaches which necessary things in particular one can learn better in communities than in solitude*

In an important treatise he wrote on society, Gregorius Capucianus, *episcopus* and learned Doctor, stated that one could acquire and learn five things in particular better within the cities and communities of this world than outside them, for in these places they are taught much more perfectly. The first, he states, are called *credenda*. And these include all that relates to the Christian faith, for there is no doubt that one can learn about the Articles of Faith and all that pertains to salvation much more easily in a fine city than one can in some other smaller town, and even less in solitude. We can see by experience that highlanders and peasants are so lacking in knowledge that they do not know how to make the sign of the cross or pray or say their confession; they know almost nothing about their faith nor about ecclesiastical statutes; it is not like this, however, in communities.

And it is from this knowledge, he says, that the second type comes, which is that of the *optanda et detestanda*, or, in other words, in large cities we are better acquainted and better informed than in solitude, where no other resides, with and about what constitutes the reward we hope to receive for our well-led lives and the torment we can expect if we have led lives that are wicked. The reason for this is that in communities and cities there are great scholars and many books, and many sermons, disputations, lessons and scholastic proceedings are continually delivered and held there which do not occur outside the great cities and communities.

The third main thing that this holy man says as to to why we must love cities and draw near to them for our enlightenment is called *vitanda*, and these are sins, for, although more sins are committed in great cities than in solitude or in small towns, nevertheless whoever wishes to avoid the opportunity for them can easily flee them wholly or in part. And he says that in the case of a man who is accustomed to teaching others, it is better or not so bad sometimes to succumb to certain straightforward sins, which as good as emerge from the conversations he has with those whom he teaches, than to abstain from those sins while one is in a state of solitude and is of no benefit to others. And he offers the following reason for this, by affirming that man is not free from sin just because he is in a state of solitude; rather, under these circumstances, his heart undergoes greater struggles and greater tempta-

tions, and in such a state there are not many refuges nor are the remedies there as plentiful as they are in communities. The heart, therefore, in solitude receives great blemishes, when God does not provide
for it by special grace; and to wait all the time for God to provide this
is not something without risk, especially for a man who is weak. For this
reason he states that, even though the man who wishes to educate himself may also be unable to refrain from sinning, he should not flee
from the city. [...]

We know, moreover, that Saint Francis asked God if his friars
should dwell in deserts or in cities, and he was told that they should
reside in cities and towns so that, through their preaching, they might
draw souls to God. And, for this reason, if it is God's will that preachers live in cities in order to teach city-dwellers how to lead a good life
in such places, then such places are more suitable and more fitting
locations for them to find out about and to appreciate their sins than
outside of society.

The fourth thing that the said Gregorius states, regarding the way
man can educate himself more easily in a city, is called *agenda*, that is
to say, knowing how one must act, whether this be towards God or
towards oneself or towards one's fellow man, for there a person is better able to educate himself in all the afore-mentioned ways than outside of society.

The fifth thing is what are called *loquenda*, that is to say, knowing
how to talk, for the man who hears other people speak in different
ways every day can learn with incomparably greater ease to speak than
he who lives in the desert and who hears no one. People, therefore,
use a common saying in this regard when they come across a coarse
person among their community, to the effect that not every ass is in
the farmyard; as if to indicate that those who live in the countryside
are like asses in their speech and in other matters.

By nothing that I have said do I wish to impugn the solitary life, since
this has been highly praised and put to the test by Our Saviour and the
holy Patriarchs, but by saying what I have, I merely wish to conclude that
cities were devised for the greater education of men and that men are
incomparably better informed and further from ignorance when living
in cities than they are in a state of solitude or in a small town. And this I
mean in general terms.

DC 12

3.4. *How the holy Church has created special posts and offices for learned men in order to educate the people*

In order, therefore, that everyone in a city has the means to educate himself, the holy mother Church has ordained, as can be seen *in quinto Decretalium, titulo De magistris,* that each cathedral church should have masters to teach those who may wish to learn Latin grammar or any other discipline that they teach, and that in their metropolitan sees there should be a theologian to teach theology, and all these should give instruction for free and ask nothing from their charges, especially the poor. And on this point the Pope ordered that the said churches should be under an obligation to assign posts to the said masters, so that they need not receive anything from the poor pupils whom they teach. And Pope Alexander decreed in this regard, under threat of severe punishment, that no one should dare to hinder that person who wishes to teach Law or another legitimate and worthy discipline so long as that teacher, however, be qualified to teach.

Trogus Pompeius said, therefore, that noble sovereigns and natural lords in particular should pay heed, so that their territories be enlightened and filled with the light of truth, to ensure that *studia specialia* pertaining to the different disciplines, especially Latin grammar, logic and philosophy, are established throughout their cities; and in a certain suitable city – or cities – within their territories, they should found *studia generalia*[16] to which their vassals might send their children in order to learn these very things, or Civil or Canon Law, or Theology or Medicine or whatever might be of greatest benefit to them. And, in order to promote knowledge, these lords must provide abundantly for the teachers in such places from their own income or privileges and must prohibit them from daring to accept anything from anyone, so that nobody should have to refrain from studying through indigence. And he states a very noteworthy teaching which has been expressed by other poets and philosophers, and the teaching is that a kingdom or city in which erudition abounds cannot be without great advantages, and that whenever and wherever there is a high level of erudition in this world, the level of chivalry in that place will automatically be high too, with the result that a high level of erudition and a high level of chivalry always go hand in hand with each other in some part of the world.

[16] That is to say, universities.*

Ovid stated that a man was perfect if he was wise, virtuous, educated and well-spoken; but if he was ignorant, lived grossly and was ill-
spoken, he said that he was brutish. If he was wise only, he said that he
was worth silver; if wise and well-spoken, he was appealing; but if he
was wise, well-spoken and virtuous he was worth more than a hundred
others and more than precious gold; and if he was only well-spoken,
he was like a fetid tomb painted on the outside. Seneca said that it was
a sign that a sovereign was becoming a tyrant, when he did not take
pleasure in wise or learned men nor foster them, for when a tyrant
sees that his vassals are learned and wise, he always fears lest by reason
of their wisdom they should kill him or that, ultimately, they should
take his lordship away from him.

DC 13

3.5. *Which states that the third main reason for building cities was in order to
avoid shameful and uncontrolled appetites*

The third main reason why cities must be built is to avoid and to free
oneself from all kinds of shameful appetites. And note here that,
although flight from temptation is one of the best remedies for avoiding evil deeds, just as we have stated above at length in various books,
however, insofar as the solitary life is the life for but very few, and the
present book deals with the sort of life that is general and common to
people, to speak right now of solitude, therefore, and to praise its
nobility would be out of place. It would not be out of place, on the
other hand, for us to teach that living in a community of note which is
well governed, as a community the size of a city must be, does more to
curb one's shameful appetites than does living in a smaller community
which is more straightforward and requires less governance, despite
the fact that in great cities or communities of note the occasions and
opportunities for sinning are much greater. And the saints have
proved on various grounds that this is the case, namely that appetites
are curbed more easily in cities and sizeable communities which are
well governed than in other, smaller places.

The first ground is this, namely that in cities man is better
acquainted with every good thing that he might wish to know, for in
such places there are more learned men, more books, more sermons,
more lectures, and more examples that are worthy from many fine
people, than there are in smaller towns, as a result of which instruc-

tion men control their appetites much more effectively than they do in an unsophisticated, small town. And, therefore, with good reason did our forefathers build great and distinguished cities in order to curb shameful appetites. [...]

Because of this that great philosopher Prometheus said that a citizen raised in a sizeable town was worth more than a citizen raised in a small town, and he recommended that peasants ensure their sons were raised in large towns and great cities if they were so able for, in such a way, they would fulfil the obligations they had towards their sons much better. For he said that, by nature, everyone should bring up and instruct his son to the best of his ability, since a son is a creature entrusted by God to a father so that he might perform as many good deeds towards him as he can, so that this son might better be prepared to serve God and the commonwealth.

Second, if a father does the contrary, a son may, with good reason, lodge a civil complaint about him and say that in this respect he has not acted like a good father but like a stranger, for he has deprived him of true wisdom and profitable knowledge, which are things that have no price in this world.

Third, since fathers, as all men, are obliged to serve the commonwealth according to their capacities, it follows that, since every person in the community is a member of that commonwealth, then every man must strive to provide it with worthy members who can be of the greatest use to it when the time is right. Since, therefore, the well-educated man can serve it better than he who is unlettered and lacking in understanding, it follows that those who are strangers to fine cities must have their sons sent to cities of note to be suitably educated, unless this is prevented by their being unable or its being impossible for them to pay for their son's studies, or by some other conceivable circumstance.

We read about Forseo, a distinguished citizen of Troy, that, when he was summoned by the court to divide his property and to give a part of it to his brothers, he replied that he would not give them any. And he did this because he said that his brothers had received many more things than he and his father had given much more to them than to him, for he had had them educated in the city of Athens, where they had been schooled in learning and in how to live, which exceeded any riches in value, whereas his father had only left him temporal goods and had always engaged him in customary matters relating to the household, just like a squire.

Facundus has written, *in sermone De gubernatione divina*, that among the other things by which God shows his noble governance is the fact that in each province he places a principal city of repute, which is a light and mirror for all the others, and in which other people from across the entire province can inform themselves about what they ought to do, say, avoid or seek out. And he gives examples of certain cities in particular, for he states that the light of Judaea was Jerusalem; the light of Egypt, Memphis; the light of Syria, Damascus; the light of Persia, Susa; the light of Mesopotamia, Edessa; the light of Africa, Carthage; the light of Greece, Athens; the lights of Germany, Strigonium,[17] Argentina[18] and Cologne; and the lights of Italy, Rome and Florence; and the light of France, Paris; and the light of the north, Godancia; the lights of Spain, Seville and Tarragona.

DC 22

4. THE TRANSLATIO STUDII[19]

4.1. *How in order to make men knowledgeable, our forefathers constructed various cities and designated various centres of study*

Since our ancestors wished to give rise to erudition and to induce every noble citizen to strive to attain true wisdom, they built various cities and gave them over to learning. And in the beginning, during the earliest years of the world, we read that the first city, called Enoch, which was constructed by Cain in the Indies, which are in in the east, was admirably endowed with great learning and erudition by Jonicus, Noah's son, whom Moses did not name in the *Bible*, according to what is stated by Saint Methodius; therefore, he says, since the said Jonicus was a virgin and a man of great virtue, he had no sons or issue at all.

And although we do not read that our first father, Adam, built a city, according to what Hugh has written, *De sacramentis, libro primo, parte* VI, *capitulo* XII, no one should doubt, however, that, with the exception of God, Adam has been the foremost sage and teacher of all wisdom and of all that is good spiritually and morally among the whole

---

[17] *Strigonium*: Esztergom, the capital of Hungary until the 13th century and the titular see of the Primate of Hungary.

[18] *Argentina*: Strasbourg.

[19] *Translatio studii*: transmission of learning.*

of humankind. And this is clear, states Hugh in this passage, if you consider who had created him and how he was fashioned by the hands of Our Lord God alone, and how also he had been enlightened by an especial rapture coming from the spirit of God in the celestial heights. Subsequently, he taught his wisdom by imposing names upon creatures according to their properties and kinds, and this likewise teaches natural reason. For, in spite of the fact that afterwards his intellect was clouded by sin, he nevertheless still retained the noble and excellent nature that God had given him and was often visited by Our Lord God, as is narrated by Scripture, and was frequently given instruction by the angelic being who watched over him. In addition, his heirs and descendents, who resorted to him as to their principal father and protector for all the doubts that befell them, required that he be a great fount of wisdom and learning, he who was a light and a governing law to other men in all their affairs and, principally, their unfailing recourse after God.

William, the famous historian who was a monk of Saint Denis of Paris,[20] recounts that, despite the fact that we do not read that our father, Adam, nor his descendents until the time of Noah, established a city, we should not doubt, however, that many of them were built in the fields of Damascus where the said saintly father of ours, Adam, was placed by Our Lord God after he was cast out of his earthly paradise. And not only may we consider that various dwellings were built there, but also throughout various other neighbouring areas. And this can be proved because, by his wisdom, our said saintly father, Adam, knew that to reside in a civic community provided its inhabitants with many opportunities to educate themselves, to protect themselves and to find consolation, all of which things were and are highly necessary to the community of men in this world, and particularly in the case of his ordering and commanding the sons of Seth, his rightful son, not to mingle with the issue of Cain, whom he realised and knew would be wicked and tainted by many iniquities, and would subsequently be scattered by God.

These very facts are true, moreover, for in his time the study of wisdom was already very widespread, which study required many people to congregate and gather together and demanded, as a consequence, great cities as well as towns and buildings. But it is clear, therefore, that during this period there was indeed such scholarly study. For he says

[20] William of Nangis, the author of a *Chronicon*, written at the end of the 13th century.

that at that time, after Enoch, son of Jared, who was born seven hundred and twenty-two years after the creation of the world, and who belonged to the seventh generation of the rightful descendents of Seth, son of Adam, had grown into an adult, he was the first to invent letters, as well as writing and the erudite arts and he made his heirs and descendents understand and study these things, and he foretold many things to come and he wrote them down, just as we read *in Epistola sancti Iudae apostoli* (Jude 1,14-15). This Enoch was the first to introduce a specific spoken office for praising almighty God. He had a son called Methuselah, whom he begot when sixty-five years of age. And, because the life of this saintly Enoch pleased Our Lord God, Moses therefore says, *Genesis* (5,24), that Our Lord God transported him to an earthly paradise, and there shall he be until the world's end, for, at that time, he is due to leave this place together with Elijah in order to preach against the evil Antichrist and to argue trenchantly against his great wickedness, as we shall be discussing at length in the *Eighth* book.

DC 15

4.2. *Which teaches by a different means what has just been said, namely that even at the beginning of the world, great cities and towns were built for the purpose of knowledge and various arts were invented*

Moreover, what is stated above, namely that at that time wisdom and knowledge of the arts had already spread across the world, is in agreement with the fact that during that period there were already various towns of note. But that such wisdom and knowledge, in fact, already took the form of arts in such times, is shown by the said historian, since he states that back then the sons of Lamech, of the line of Cain, invented and practised certain arts.

First of all Jabal, the first son of Lamech, was a shepherd and devised the art of making tents in which shepherds could live and which they could move when the shepherds changed the pasture of their flocks. This son, the author says, was the first to separate the sheep from the goats and to arrange for each species to graze in distinct flocks. He was also the first to think up a way of marking one's flock with a particular sign, so that it might be told apart when someone wished to separate one from the other.

The second son of Lamech was called Jubal, and he invented musical instruments, such as the organ, the viola and the rebec, and

other stringed instruments, although later on many others were
devised. And he contrived and made these for the entertainment of
the shepherds who lived alone watching over their flocks. And the
Master of Histories says that this Jubal learnt to produce these har-
monies as a result of the melodious sounds that he heard being emitted by the hammers of one of his brothers, called Tubalcain, who
made use of blacksmith's tools and various hammers with which his
servants often beat upon the anvil. Certain people likewise say that he
was strongly inspired to do this as a result of his finding a dead and
overturned tortoise, from which the birds had eaten all of the flesh
within and left its nerves, which nerves had dried out and become
taut; and when the wind blew some grass which lay across the said
dried-out tortoise, and, being stirred, that grass touched the said
dried and taut nerves, it made a sound resembling the strings of a
lute, and this inspired him to make stringed instruments.

Lamech's third son was called Tubalcain, and this son invented the
art of metalwork and he made weapons. And Peter Comestor says that
he discovered it as follows, namely that when he was making a fire in
the wood where his flock was, a wood in which there were different
kinds of metal, he saw that the metal was melted by the fire and, once
melted, it assumed the form of the place where it had fallen. And then
he realised that he could do what he wished with metals, using the
strength of fire; for this reason, then, he did what he wished with
them, all in the service of man.

Lamech's fourth child was a daughter, named Noema, and she
contrived the art of weaving, and she based her discovery upon the
weaving of spiders, according to what Peter Comestor says. And note
here that the children of Cain invented the arts pertaining to man's
physical comfort and to temporal wealth. On the basis of these said
arts and of many others which were devised at that time, Etnicus
wishes to prove that there were already in those days various significant
buildings and communities. For he states that human guile enables
whatever is bad to become worse; and those tents which were first
devised inspired men to build houses in order better to have repose.
And musical instruments excited the flesh and, as a result, such excite-
ment required a suitable building. So likewise the art of metalwork
required a building, and its principal purpose, which was to make
weapons, required that men who had learnt and were familiar with the
art of fighting battles should congregate together, men who had need

of a safe place where they could live and might have shelter and succour. And likewise to make cloth and to weave required the very same.
So it is clear that men already had at that time certain noteworthy
buildings and places where they lived, which were towns and cities and
settlements of this type.

And Peter Comestor[21] proves this very point, for he says that it was
then the year one thousand six hundred and fifty-six since the creation
of the world, and Seth's progeny, who were called the children of
God, had become mingled by marriage and by fornication with Cain's
progeny, who were called the offspring of Man, against the decree and
ordinances given by the first great patriarch, Adam, who was already
dead. And as a result of this mingling the world had arrived at such a
revolting state by its extreme excesses of lust, which could be seen
among women in particular, that, at that time, Our Lord God sent that
holy man, Noah, to preach to all the peoples of the world by announc-
ing the wrath of God to them, a wrath which would shortly be upon all
of mankind if it did not mend its sinful ways. And he proclaimed to
them, on behalf of Our Lord God, that the lives of men could last for
no longer than a hundred and twenty years from that point forwards
or, in other words, if they did not mend their vile ways, then the whole
world would perish in a deluge after a hundred and twenty years.
Therefore, says this author, it is certain that if Noah should have had
to seek out men one by one throughout the world in order to tell them
what has just been said, the purpose of his travels would never have
been achieved and, therefore, it was fitting that he should find them
in large and significant settlements, where he proclaimed the said
divine judgement.

And Peter Comestor says, in this respect, that, as certain distinguished men gave credence to Noah's preaching and believed that
the world would perish just as he had said, since they realised that
people did not wish to mend their ways, therefore, he says, they wrote
down the arts and sciences which they knew and had invented with
great difficulty; and so that they should not be lost or remain
unknown to the men of the future, they inscribed them upon two
great pillars. And they made one from stone so that it could not be
destroyed by water, and the other from clay so that, in case the world
was destroyed by fire, it would not be burnt or ruined. And they say
that the stone pillar still stands firm in the area of Syria, and on

---

[21] *Historia scholastica. Liber Genesis*, chap. XXXI.

account of this structure some wish to say and to conclude that it was necessary, in those days, for there to have been significant communities in order for them to have carried out and recommended such things for the benefit of the human race and to have acquired them by such varied and erudite study so as to instruct mankind.

DC 16

4.3. *Which demonstrates the same point by another means*

In order to demonstrate this same point, certain people adduce a saying of Josephus who reports that Manassah of Damascus, a distinguished historian, states in book LXXXIX of his *Antiquities*[22] that in Armenia there was an extremely high mountain, called Paris. And he says that, in that place, there were, during the time of the Flood, dwellings and a community of people, which were not reached by the prevailing waters of the Flood. So, it is clear that, in those days, there were communities of people not only on the plains, but also in the mountains.

And second, because, as Josephus says,[23] such was the profundity of the arts and sciences invented by our fathers from this early period, that nobody should doubt the great and long life that is attributed to them by Holy Scripture. For he says that, if only to learn the celestial course of the Greatest Year,[24] an astrologer who wished to have experience of this would have to live for six hundred years, for within such a span do the planets return to the first place in which they were created, according to what he says. And those who wrote the first ancient accounts concerning the Egyptians and the Greeks, such as Mamenot, who wrote of the deeds of the Egyptians, and Berosus, who wrote down the sayings of the Chaldeans, and many others, bear witness to this. Therefore, say these writers, since the acquisition of great erudition and the painstaking assembly of different books and arts requires debate and lengthy discussion by many learned men who study and live together, it is clear that in those times there were already such communities, and this was the case because these latter were essential to the experts and the experts to them, in accordance with what we have already referred to above.

[22] *Antiquitates Iudaicae* I, 93.
[23] *Antiquitates Iudaicae* I, 104.
[24] Not the Platonic year (25,800 years) but the *annus magnus* of Josephus (600 years).*

The *History of the East*[25] recounts that Olympius, a famous shepherd in Palestine, built ten cities in Syria in order to bring together
there all the men who were scattered throughout various solitary
houses across that entire region. And he gave an order, on the recommendation of other distinguished people who were famous in the earliest years of the world, that, under pain of exile, all the inhabitants of
the said cities were obliged to know the following things by the end
of their first year of residence, namely who God is and what He asks of
men, what men's obligations to Him are and what man has to do for
himself if he wishes to be saved, as well as what obligations man has
towards his fellow men, in particular, and towards the community, in
general. He prescribed, in addition, that, in the said cities, there
should always be teachers of those arts which had already been
invented at that time and that there should be large *studia* or universities in which everyone was obliged, under that same pain, to ensure
that his son received at least three years instruction so that no one
there was ignorant. He decreed that whoever did not wish to acquire
such knowledge could not be noble, nor could he occupy a position of
governance over the community, nor could he dare to claim any pre-
eminence or honour among experts. And he stated that he wished his
people to adhere to such ordinances because he said that an ignorant
man is nothing but a brute, and compared to the learned man he is
darkness as to light and earth as to sky, unless the nobility of a virtuous
life and of excellent morals should warrant reversing the order, so that
the virtuous man preceded the one who was learned. Because of this,
it states here that he required small children to be taught good manners and habits, before, during, and after they had devoted themselves
to learning. It states, therefore, that in his time there was a variety of
people conspicuous for their virtuous lives and their knowledge of the
different sciences throughout Syria and its various other neighbouring
regions, and in these places they devised a number of mechanical and
contemplative arts.

DC 17

---

[25] *History of the East*: this probably refers to the *Historia orientalis* by Jacques de Vitry.*

4.4. Which states how, in the world's second age, various kingdoms, cities and universities sprang up

In the world's second age, men began to establish kingdoms and, as a consequence, they built many cities and ennobled them with various universities and with different teachings and disciplines, so that their citizens should be people of learning, good counsel and sound governance, and such that through their learning and goodness these kingdoms and kings might receive worthy guidance and the cities be well governed, as we read in the histories of old.

The first king there ever was, who in those times became the first lord of men through his peculiar tyranny, was called Nimrod. This king was a terrible giant and a mighty and evil man, and he was the son of Itari[26] and nephew of Eber, and was born in the year one thousand eight hundred and fifty-seven, counting from the date of the world's creation. This Nimrod was descended from Ham and, desiring to exalt himself, according to the words of Comestor,[27] he departed after the death of Noah to the great land of Shinar and there he built the city of Babylon and that tower known as Babel, which means confusion, for in that place were languages confounded, for, since all men had formerly spoken a single language, from then on were they split into seventy-two. Nimrod, in order to ennoble the said city, inscribed two pillars with astrological and geometrical lore, one of which was made of metal and the other of brick, and he did this so that the said pillars should be destroyed by neither flood nor flame nor should those sciences perish. This Nimrod had eight sons, one of whom was called Belus, and this son succeeded him in the kingdom of Babylon. And he had another son, called Cres, who went away with other men to the island of Crete, where he was the first king and imposed his name upon the island, and favoured it with a good deal of veritable wisdom. He also built cities and towns there and enlightened them with his considerable learning, although the *Roman History* states that the said Nimrod was persecuted and cast out of Babylon and fled to the said island of Crete, and there died. And then the people of Babylon chose a new king for themselves.

DC 18

---

[26] He was, in fact, the son of Chus, Kush or Csh.*
[27] Cf. Peter Comestor, *Historia scholastica. Liber Genesis*, chap. XXXVIII.

4.5. *Which describes the beginning of the kingdom of the Goths and how the philosopher, Zenta, helped at that time to spread knowledge northwards*

On the nineteenth centenary of the creation of the world began the kingdom of the Goths. These people were begot by Magog, son of Japheth, which Japheth was the son of Noah. And from him were begot the Hungars, the Vandals and those from the kingdom of Sweden. And the historian, Rodericus,[28] says in this respect that these people inhabited the lands to the north of the Black Sea, and they located their principal site in the first province of Europe travelling towards the east, a province called Sicia,[29] which stretches as far as the great Danube river and up to Germany. These Goths spread out towards the west and made Dacia[30] the centre of their kingdom, in honour of which and for the benefit of whose lands they chose a great philosopher called Zenta as their king, who greatly enhanced, endowed and dignified their territories by his great knowledge and learning. And castles, towns and cities cannot easily be built on that land, as the region is very marshy, but they set up movable cities, that is to say, cities made of tents that they carry upon carts, and they move from place to place according to what they think the weather is going to be like.

DC 19

4.6. *How the study of wisdom came to Egypt and, later, to Greece*

Eusebius states that during this period of the kingdom of the Sicians and the Goths, that of Egypt grew up. In order to preserve this kingdom, King Epaphus, the son of Jupiter, built there a notable city called Memphis, and in that place there was a great school of mathematics, according to what Isidorus states, XV *Ethymologiarum, capitulo primo*. And Pythagoras and the great Plato went there to acquire wisdom, according to what Saint Jerome says in his Prologue to the *Bible, capitulo primo*. Once Cambyses, king of the Persians, had obtained the kingdom of Egypt, he gave it the name of Babylon-in-Egypt, and it is now called Cairo, where the Sultan usually resides. At that time, this

---

[28] Rodericus Ximenes de Rada, *Historia gothica* I, 10.

[29] More probably Scythia, known to the Goths as Oium, meaning "in the waterlands", although Bartolomaeus Anglicus, in his *De proprietatibus rerum* XV, 147, refers to Sicia as that region covering Eastern Europe and Asia Minor, from the Danube to Germania.*

[30] *Dacia*: territory covering Romania and parts of Hungary.

kingdom possessed such great knowledge that it enlightened almost the entire world in its day, for Ptolemy, the great astrologer and sovereign of that art, who wrote such marvellous books on astrology, emerged therefrom. And you must note in this respect that, according to what the Master of Histories states, Abiathar, the supreme bishop of Jerusalem, sent Ptolemy, the king of Egypt, at the latter's request, seventy interpreters to explain the *Bible*[31] to him painstakingly in his own language. And there the said Ptolemy built up such a notable library containing all types of books that the world had never seen its like. So wisdom and knowledge issued forth from this kingdom and passed to the Greeks and various other nations. This kingdom lasted until the time of Octavian, who was the emperor called Caesar Augustus. But it is true that it was immediately brought to a halt by certain circumstances and persecutions which militated against it.

DC 20

4.7. *How, after this, cities and universities multiplied throughout the world*

In this very same period Noah's son, Ham, who is called Zoroaster by another name, reigned in a province of Asia Minor known as Bactria. And, in order to ennoble his kingdom, Ham devoted himself to various kinds of knowledge, both good and evil. And he was born laughing, which fact, Saint Augustine has stated, did not portend well for him.[32] And he inscribed the seven liberal arts onto seven metal and seven earthen columns, so that the said arts should be preserved against any deluge of water and from any outbreak of fire. Elinandus says that some of the sayings of the said Ham came into the hands of Aristotle, who subsequently expanded upon and made marvels of them. After this came some of the principal empires, such as that of Persia, and afterwards came the kingdom of Solomon and of his heirs. And all these people caused wisdom and knowledge to increase to a very high degree. And Solomon, in particular, established an outstanding school for all the arts in Jerusalem and there, in his day, did he conduct disputes and teach men knowledge and wisdom in a great variety of ways.

After this, monarchy came to the Greeks, for which reason, at that time, there was a singular flourishing of wisdom and knowledge there

[31] Cf. Peter Comestor, *Historia scholastica. Liber Genesis*, chap. XV, additio 1.
[32] Cf. *De civitate Dei* XXI, 14.

in their study of lofty, heavenly matters in addition to the philosophical. Later on there were distinguished legislators in that place, influential philosophers who were the light of the world, among whom the
most celebrated were Thales Milesius, Anaximander, Anaxagoras,
Archelaus, Socrates, Plato and Aristotle.[33] And from there the empire
passed to the Romans, as a consequence of which did they at once
establish the principal centre of study for all kinds of knowledge in
Rome, for there did they deal in particular with laws and all types of
philosophy, and even with God and theology, to the degree that their
capacity for reason could attain. And at that time there flourished
among them innumerable poets and various ladies inspired by God to
speak in the spirit of prophecy, ladies who were called Sybils. And from
there, after the construction of Paris in France, this knowledge and
study of wisdom arrived here, and from here it passed to England,
where there are various, notable universities, and after the said places
it has been spread throughout the entire world.

See then how knowledge arises from great buildings and from
towns and cities, and this is so by special order of Our Lord God, so
that cities might be special places which are more suited than all
others to driving men away from every kind of ignorance and to letting them know what is necessary to their bodies and souls.

DC 21

4.8. *How the learned philosophers of old have belonged to various estates*

Speaking about the condition of the said philosophers, Alexander of
Neckam, *libro De naturis rerum* (II, 174), says that there were some who
roamed across the world, such as Abraham, of whom he says that he
learnt the afore-mentioned quadrivial arts in Egypt. There have been
others who were sovereigns, such as the great Alexander and Julius
Caesar, Nero, Tiberius and Ptolemy, *rex Egipti*, and Alfonso, king of
Spain, who drew up the Alfonsine Tables. And he says that whenever
sovereigns have been great philosophers, they have performed great
wonders in their territories, and he says that it is rightful that it should
be so because wisdom teaches knights what they must do and kings
how they must govern. Divine wisdom states, therefore, *Proverbiorum*
VIII: *Per me reges regnant* (8,15), and it means that the reigns of kings
who govern well on its account shall be felicitous.

33 Eiximenis is following *De civitate Dei* VIII, 2-4.

There have been others who were ordinary citizens, as were the
seven wise men of Athens, who were like seven stars illuminating the
world, and later on there have been philosophers in that very place
and in Rome who were highly distinguished citizens, and later in Paris,
according to what Elinandus says in his chronicle, where he states that,
when Charlemagne reigned there, Alcuin transferred the great university in Rome to Paris, and thus will you find it in the book called *Speculum*.[34] And, as Tullius says, the heavenly God has caused wisdom to
descend and has placed it in the famous cities, such as Athens, in
Greece; Rome, in Italy; Paris, in France, and, generally, in all those
cities where there reside learned and informed people who live righteous and virtuous lives in accordance with the divine laws and commandments of Christians.

DC 191

---

34 Vincent of Beauvais, *Speculum historiale* XXIII, 173.

EDUCATION IN THE HOME

II

1. PARENTS AND CHILDREN

1.1. *Why and to what extent parents must take particular care of their children*

It suffices for sovereigns to take care of their children when they are born, and subsequently when they are somewhat older and also until they have left their tutelage. And they must take such care by first thinking that children are the product and offspring of their father after God, for it is the concern of all who produce anything to love, preserve and sustain what they have produced so that it might flourish and prosper. We can see that the birds, the beasts and the fish do this, and every kind of creature loves, cherishes, fosters and maintains the welfare of its progeny.

Second, because nature has charged fathers and mothers with the care of their children. Third, because Aristotle proves, VIII *Ethicorum*,[1] that every lover is especially attentive towards the thing that he loves. And since Our Lord God has filled the hearts of fathers and mothers with love for their children, therefore, they must take special care of them. And he notes in this regard that, although by nature everyone loves his child, certain philosophers, however, have given reasons why nature is so inclined. And they say that the first reason is that a son is the natural product of the father and, by nature, every producer loves what he has produced, and just as nature drives man to beget, so also it drives him to love what he has begotten. The second reason is because a son is the likeness of his father, for Aristotle states that each

[1] Cf. *Ethica ad Nicomachum* VIII, 1.

thing begets its like,[2] and by nature loves its like, as we read in *Ecclesiasticus* XIII (19-20).[3] And since sons resemble their fathers in nature, for they are men just like them, then fathers must love them and on account of this love must be diligent in their care of them. The third reason is because fathers grow weak and, by nature, wish to perpetuate themselves yet cannot, since they draw near to death, thus they perpetuate themselves through their sons. We read, therefore, in *Ecclesiasticus* XXX that man dies yet he is not dead, for his son remains, who is another father himself (30,4). The fourth reason is because everyone is said to be perfect, according to the Philosopher, when he is able to beget himself; thus sons bear witness to the disclosure of their fathers' perfection and, as a consequence, fathers love them as testimony to their own perfection.[4]

From all this it is clear that parents must be attentive out of love and not because of the services they expect from their children; from which it follows that children are to be governed in one way and housemaids and servants in quite another, which latter are governed with severity and fear, and not with love.

DC 551

1.2. *Women and children*

The first reason why Our Lord God made woman was to provide company for man. And this is proved by what is contained in the book called *Genesis*, which is concerned with the creation of the world, and in which Moses states at the beginning that Our Lord God said, after he had created Adam: "It is not good that man should be alone. Let us make him a helper and companion, then, who is like unto him" (2,18). And then he made woman. [...]

The second reason why woman is made in such female kind is for the multiplication of human nature, for it pleased Our Lord God that the human race was not all created at the same time at the beginning of the world, as were the angels, but rather that men were begotten by man and woman in whom and through whom the said begetting took place. [...]

---

   2 *Ethica ad Nicomachum* VIII, 1.
   3 Chapter and verse of the Latin Vulgate. In modern Roman Catholic Bibles, this passage is to be found in *Sirach* (i.e. *Ecclesiasticus*) 13,15.*
   4 All these ideas have their origin in the *Ethica ad Nicomachum* VIII, 7.

The third reason why woman was given as a companion to man, states this writer, was so as to nurture children, for women do this much better than men by divine ordinance, with the result that it is quite natural for a woman to be inclined to nurture children. And this is the reason why small girls make themselves dolls from fabric or from wood and act as if they are suckling them and treat them just as if they were alive and were their own children.

LD 6

2. THE EDUCATION OF CHILDREN

2.1. *The obligations of parents towards their children*

Chapter CXLVIII, which describes the fourth lucrative kind, which is a special art and occupation

The fourth way of earning money is called artistic. And this is the ability to earn money by some lucrative art or by one's worldly occupation as lord or in the community. The arts which are more lucrative than others are those of the jurist, the doctor, the money changer, the minter, the merchant and the lawyer, when there are few of these, as there should be, except in the case of merchants.

Every man must pass on to his son the very best profession he can, according to what the philosopher Zeno said. For this reason he said that a son may always express a grievance against his father in the following matters, that is to say, first, if he is not his legitimate son or if he does not acknowledge him as such. Second, if he gives him a horrible name. Third, if he has brought him up badly. Fourth, if he has forgotten to give him the paternal, necessary and natural privileges that are due to him. Fifth, if he has taught him an unprofitable way of life, for everyone can teach his son some worthy profession which is good in itself or is in accordance with the ways and customs of his country.

Likewise, to hold the position of lord, especially a position in a household, such as being Chancellor, Vice-Chancellor, Treasurer, Keeper of the Privy Purse, Chamberlain, Steward, Keeper of the King's or Lord's Wardrobe, Lord Justice, Protonotary or Secretary. All of these are lucrative offices. Likewise, to hold any administrative office outside the household of a lord is lucrative and respectable.

Likewise, all the wordly arts, whatever they be, are given over to making money in order to earn one's livelihood, for the art of chivalry, in the case of the one who exercises it, is given over likewise to this, even though the community ordains that it be for the protection of the commonwealth. This art then, if carried out with prudence and audacity, is most respectable and merits great rewards in money and in other good things, especially civic and political honours.

DC 148

2.2. *The right path*

2.2.1. *How, in order to avoid the said ill-treatment, fathers and mothers must not be overfamiliar with their children*

The desire, moreover, to forestall this contempt should spur natural fathers, above all, and then mothers, to avoid showing too much flattery or familiarity towards their children, for if they act in this way, their children do not fear them and become even worse. However, whatever the mother does, the father must strictly observe this rule, for he should always show only a small degree of familiarity to his son and should speak to him only a little, and his words should be severe, though restrained, and not excessive, for Saint Paul says: *Nolite esse amari filiis vestris.*[5] And, addressing those who have children, he means the following: Do not be unduly harsh or insufferable towards your children, so that you do not drive them to despair for, if you do so, you will fall into the trap you wish to avoid, namely that they should hold you in contempt for, if children see their parents being cruel to them, they will leave them and take a different path. And you must bear this in mind with regard to children who are already older, for one must treat such children in a more friendly manner than the little ones who do not possess good sense, though also maintaining all the while the due authority of fathers over their children and the due reverence of children towards their fathers.

Likewise, every lord must behave similarly towards the subjects within his household and outside it, although great distinctions must be made between one subject and another, and between one vassal and another; however, at all times must due reverence towards a lord be observed, which reverence will never be shown him if he is too

5 Eiximenis confuses two verses from Saint Paul, namely Col 3,19 and 3,21.

familiar with his household servants. For this reason, he must never joke or play with his servants, nor must he permit his servants to dare to do or say anything in his presence which is not as it should be or, if he so permits, he should not be there nor should anyone dare to say anything of this nature in front of him. Every lord who wishes to be held in esteem must let his servants and his subjects know that the evils that he allows to be committed are matters unknown to him and that, if indeed they were known, he would not tolerate them for anything in the world. And in this manner everyone takes care then that, if he commits an indiscretion, he keep it a secret.

In the same way, a teacher must never be very familiar with his pupils, but rather whenever he sees them, and however much they learn, he must reprimand them for learning little and for having scant sense and a meagre knowledge of God. And for this reason the said teacher must never allow his pupils to know that he is satisfied with their progress for, if he permits this, they will swell with pride at this news and will show contempt for their teacher's commands and later for his very person.

TC 132

2.2.2. *Against disreputable company*

The second point is that everyone must avoid disreputable company at all costs. The reason for this is because, as Ciprianus says, *epistola nona*, poor company corrupts others in the following ways: the first is that such company always begets wickedness which, when repeated in front of another, exerts a heavy allure and attraction upon the mind of the person who witnesses it; the second is that intrinsically our natures are strongly disposed to letting in all kinds of corruption when there is a place and time and propitious occasion for it; the third is that bad company results in profane language which corrupts good morals, according to what Saint Paul says, *I Corintiorum* (15,33); the fourth is that on the whole everyone wishes to please the other and, as a consequence, if a person sees that by acting wickedly he can please that other, he will immediately do as that person wishes. For this reason, Seneca said not to approach a wicked man if you do not wish to be wicked, for just as a leprous body taints others, so also does an evil man taint those who are readily at his side. [...] King David said: *Cum sancto sanctus eris et cum perverso perverteris* (Ps 17,26-27). And he means that if you remain with the holy man you shall be holy, and with the perverse and evil man you shall be perverse and evil. As the common saying goes: "Tell me about those with whom you can be found and I shall tell you whither your deeds are bound." [...]

The *History of Africa* recounts that Asser, teacher of Pompia, who was Duke of Garb, corrupted a child with his wicked advice and disreputable company into doing and saying all manner of evil things.[6] And it states in this respect that among the other things that he taught the young fellow was to have a very marked sweet tooth and always gladly to be in the kitchen and to smack his lips whilst eating. He also taught him, if he were to find someone eating, to shout out to him in a loud voice in front of everybody and say, "Oh, I hope it makes you sick!" And if someone were to sneeze, he was to call out loudly to him "Curse you!" And if anyone were to stumble against something, again he was to say to him "Have a good trip!" And an endless number of similarly wicked things. And since the young lad had passed his vices on to many other young people, and the said boy stood before the father of the said Duke while the said father was eating, and certain of the said young lads had entered the dining hall where he was eating, they shouted out that they hoped that it made him sick, whereupon he choked. And when he sneezed they called out to him in loud voices "Curse you!" and other such base things, whereupon the said sovereign knew that all those children had been led astray by the bad company they had kept with the boy to whom the said Asser had set such a poor example by his wicked teachings. He then ordered the said Asser to be sent into exile for ever more away from Africa entirely, and he ordered all the children who had thus been lead astray to live on the island of Malta for as long as it took to cure them of their vices. And then he imposed a strict law upon all parents that they should protect their children from disreputable company.

DC 808

---

[6] Unidentifiable personage and locations. Asser and Garb (or Asher and Gad), of course, are two of the twelve Patriarchs and sons of the Biblical Jacob.*

2.3. *The wrong path*

2.3.1. *The man who does not raise his children well, invariably sounds his own death knell*

The second piece of advice that the said Gregory wrote to the said sovereign stated that quick-witted children should be raised in the common fashion, for Evandrius said that a child who is raised in the common fashion rather than in an indulgent manner has had his life saved, for indulgence is the gateway to death and a terrible burden upon the one who bears it.

The third states that they should be raised shrewdly, for, as Tullius says, *libro secundo De tusculanis questionibus*, this is, in fact, the true legacy that fathers and mothers leave their children if they have brought them up to live a good life. Therefore, the philosopher Lopartas, writing to the Elamites, said that this was the reason so many of their children were dying, for they were bringing them up improperly. [...] Oh! And of how many does Valerius speak, *libro quinto, capitulo* VIII, who killed their children because they saw how disobedient they were, saying that it was better to live without children than always to have wayward children round one's neck and to be witness to one's own misery and shame! And Saint Augustine, V *De civitate Dei, capitulo* XVIII, speaks of this very matter at length.

Look how the High Priest Eli died as a result of his wicked sons, and in what misery he lived when he realised that they were dead, for he knew that on account of their sins God had withdrawn all pontifical honours for ever more from his family, as we read in the *First Book of Kings* (1 Sam 4,12-18). See likewise, in this very place, how Samuel, the holy prophet, had his judgeship over that people withdrawn because his sons were unprincipled (1 Sam 8). See in the *Second Book of Kings* how that saintly man David lived in such sorrow and danger on account of his wicked sons (2 Sam 13-18). And, in general, hold to be true that saying of the holy abbot Abdon, who said to Romelen, king of Cairo, that the man who does not raise his children well, invariably sounds his own death knell.

Oh! How many authorities will you find in Holy Scripture on this subject! Countless, for sure, just as you will find in the *Seventh* book dealing with the Fourth Commandment of God's law; all of which, taken together, mean that if you raise your children well and do not spare them from the rod and from correction, you will have pleasure and joy from them; but if you are too easy on them and let them do as they please, God shall cause you to live in sorrow and shame on their account before you die, and they shall cause your life to be shortened. Tullius, in his *De officiis*, comments upon the madness of men, who see how the birds and beasts take great care to protect their children from all kinds of troubles – for the eagle, in particular, positions its young in high spots to which nothing can draw near, and places precious stones in its nest to protect them from young egg thieves, and it brings them up so morally that, if they cannot or know not how to look at the sun directly, it casts them out of the nest at once – and yet men, infatuated by the filial love of their children, laugh at all their follies and light-mindedness, whereas they ought to consider that the primary goal that man must have, should be to raise his children in the service of God.

DC 790

2.3.2. *Parents must not give too much to their children*

Gundissalinus, however, in his *De informatione civium*, gives the following advice to parents in this regard, and it is this, namely that you should not give so much to your children while you are alive that subsequently you need to court their generosity or that you have to undergo distress, poverty or hardship on their account. It is great folly, said this writer, to place oneself at risk of despair or to be laid out on account of any filial love. An ancient law of the noble king, Ligurgus, stated that any gift made by a father to his son during his lifetime could be revoked at any time by the sovereign, so long as the father who made this gift was still alive. And, as the time-worn saying goes, he who rewards his sons too roundly deserves to be struck on the head most soundly.

We read about Aubeterre of Bordeaux that, since his son no longer paid heed to him once he had given him his inheritance, one of his father's friends, in agreement with the said father himself, made sure that the son was accused of murder. And that same friend said these words to the son:

"Relinquish or make a gift of all you have received from your father so that the court does not confiscate all you possess, for your father is already elderly and cannot keep hold of it for very long, nor does he have anyone to give it to but you."

And the son did just this and, once this had been done, his father took back all his possessions and the charge of murder did not proceed any further for, since it was a matter of invention, nobody went on with it. And, for this reason, the son returned to his house and the father forcibly ejected him, and disinherited him and caused him to die in great distress, just as the son had made his father live in great distress.

In Seville, Ferdinand of Malta had a father who had bequeathed great riches to him, and he forced him to wear shabby clothing and to live in extremely miserable conditions. And the said Ferdinand had a young son, which son, having been persuaded by the grandfather, implored his father to make a long tunic for his own father with which he might cover himself. And the father, out of love for his son, made it for him from a very poor length of cloth, from which two ells[7] were left over. And when the tunic was ready, the son spoke the following words to his father:

"Father, I pray you, please give me that cloth."[8]

And the father replied:

"And what will you do with it?"

To which the son replied:

"I shall keep it until you are as old as my grandfather, and then I shall give it to you to use as a short and pitiful tunic, and I shall give it to you with ill grace and grudgingly just as you have done right now to this grandfather of mine and father of yours."

And the said Ferdinand acknowledged his great error and said:

"Blessed be Our Lord, Who by the words of this child has decided so mercifully to correct my fault."

And from that moment on he treated his father nobly, as was the duty of a good son.

DC 792

2.3.3. *Widows tend to bring up their children badly*

Likewise, Ambrosius says that a married woman who is living with a bad husband must consider herself a widow and must lead the life of a good widow, for in that case she has the rewards of marriage and of widowhood all in one. And there are many whom God has elected to

---

7 An ell is a measure of length equal to the distance between the hand and the elbow.*

8 The cloth which the son demands from the father is the two ells left over after making the tunic.

this estate in order to test their patience and the prudence of their conduct, many, that is to say, for whom a great recompense awaits in the Kingdom of God. Likewise, he says in another place that a widow who is left with children is the mother of orphans and plays the role of father and mother at the same time, and she will receive the reward in heaven reserved for both parties if she raises them in God above all else. But widows are wont to bring up their children badly, inasmuch as an ill-mannered child is usually known as a widow's nursling and, for this reason, God already punishes them in this life, for those children that they have brought up badly pull out their eyes while they are still alive and have little recollection of them after they have died, whereas they could have won a glorious crown in Paradise if they had raised their children well.

LD 100

2.3.4. *An example of a son spoiled by his mother*

And here the chronicle tells us that this king of Sheba had a son who was easily aroused to repugnance, so that they could not give him a bowl, a plate or a cup which pleased him, but instead almost everything summoned up revulsion in him. And his father, who had learnt of this, said to him:

"Judging by the signals that you are giving, you are not my son, for I am a scrupulous man, yet I am able and willing to undertake and undergo just about anything, but everything sickens and disgusts you. So, for this reason, if you do not wish me to kill you, leave my kingdom and go where you will, for I intend to make your brother king, who seems to me to be an upstanding figure in every respect."

And the chronicle states that this son, who saw how angry his father was and that, doubtless, he would do what he had said, realised the great dangers and harm that would befall him in the matter of the threats his father had made to him, and replied thus:

"My Lord, until today I have been a child and I have wished to please my mother, who detests things most readily and takes great pleasure in my own turns of abhorrence, saying that I resemble her closely. However, from here on I wish to demonstrate to you that I am like you in every respect, and that I do not by any means feel disgusted of my own volition, but that everything I display in this relation, I have done in order to please my mother, believing that it would not displease you. But so that you believe that I am telling you the truth, in other words that I am not inclined to feel disgust at all, I wish continually to eat, drink and lie amongst swine in front of you for as long as it should please you, and I wish to kiss, serve and embrace lepers until you can see clearly that I am sickened by nothing in this world save that which displeases you."

And in the presence of his father, this son immediately sat down amidst swine and did what he had said. And his father suddenly changed his mind, and named him as his first-born heir and loved him more than ever. And he said:

"Neither should sovereigns nor men of noble line be too demanding, nor should men be easily aroused to repugnance, but rather should they be ready for anything, without exception, in spite of everything, and in all respects."

Pay heed, says the chronicle at this point, to the efforts this young man had to make to overcome himself so as not to forfeit his inheritance. For sure, nobody who has made such an effort to attain any virtue has not suddenly become virtuous.

DC 528

3. ON CHASTISEMENT

3.1. *The need for chastisement*

Which describes the ninth holy angelic service, which is to reprimand those who err

Ciprianus states in this respect, therefore, that in olden times parents and even great sovereigns were in the habit of selecting certain prudent and scrupulous men to whom they gave the job of taking them to task for their vices while, however, keeping to all the proper conventions, that is to say, of time, place and other circumstances which might remove all scandal from their being called to account. And he says on this topic, that if anyone abhors being brought to book, it is a sign of his madness, pride and wickedness, and shows that he does not know what is good for him nor does he value greatly his own salvation; but rather, Ciprianus says, such men loathe Our Lord with a vengeance and often Our Lord leads them to a sorry end. And he says also that adults must reprimand the young, and that if, through lack of chastisement, the young person or subject sins or is lost, Our Lord will settle the score for this condemned soul with his prelate or the adult. Moreover, he says that equal must reprove equal, according to what Our Saviour teaches, *Matthew* XVIII,15-17, through His detailed instruction that, first, it must be dealt with secretly, then in front of witnesses, and then it must be communicated to the ruler. Similarly, younger people must take their elders to task, and in this way did Saint Peter reprehend Saint Paul, who obliged the Jews who had converted to Christianity to revert to Judaism. And if all adults were to err, chastisement would fall by necessity to the young for then the young would be superior in this regard, just as every believer is superior to every misbeliever and heretic, and every righteous person is superior in a certain respect to every person who errs, in that very respect according to which he errs.

At the end of the said homily, the aforesaid Doctor states that he knew for sure that it was revealed by God's holy angel to a reverend and very devout man that many lords and many subjects were damned through lack of chastisement, and this only happens because lords treat their subjects in too kindly a manner and prefer to receive favours, honours and worldly goods from them than to see these subjects living good and virtuous lives. In the same way, many are damned because they do not accept correction nor desire it. Blood parents, in particular, are often damned for, blinded by their love of their offspring, they do not take care to punish or to reprimand their children and, for this reason, God wishes that they should never have pleasure from them here and, afterwards, that, in death, the damnable and immoral lives of their children might tellingly incriminate them before God, as is also the case with those who are on the way to perdition on account of the great fault of their parents, who have neither punished nor told them off nor instructed them in the ways of God. Likewise, if children do not accept reproofs from their parents with all due reverence, the aforesaid irreverence will lead them to perdition and their parents are excused by God.

LA 53

3.2. *Better are the blows of a friend than the honeyed words of a flatterer*

When the famous patriarch Victorinus was writing to Euphronius, king of Lombardy, and was telling him that a sovereign must be patient, he said the following in one of his letters:

"Pay heed to the great sovereigns of old and see how their lives remind you to be patient and to bide your time in all things, for the great Jesus, son of Sirach, said as much, *Ecclesiastici primo: Usque ad tempus sustinebit patiens* (1,29), that is to say, that a patient man shall always endure until the right moment. And the worthy sovereign must hold out until the moment when he who is invading or has already mounted an offensive commits such a great excess that justice demands that he be opposed, or when his invasion is so forceful that whoever does not oppose him could not forbear it without great danger." [...] Similarly, we read of wonders in the case of the great Christian emperors of old, particularly that of Justin who, when a friend of his took him aside and spoke to him of grave outrages and one of his servants asked him how he could bear it, replied:

"If I were not to forbear it, I should not be a man, but a beast who does not pay heed to reason, for the man who possesses reason must always be patient towards God, and towards his teacher, his chastiser, his friend, his father, and his mother, for each of these speaks out of love. And better are the blows of a friend than the honeyed words of a flatterer, according to what Scripture says."

DC 615

3.3. *Against chastisement in anger*

Experience teaches that everyone would sooner let himself be chastised and told what to do by a kindly than by a violent, proud and haughty man. For this reason David says: *Superveniet mansuetudo et corripiemur* (Ps 89,10). And he meant that there where kindliness reigns do those subjects who are worthy let themselves be chastised, for the gentle ways of kindliness warrant this. And Seneca says that the heart of man is noble by nature and will not let itself be subjected to force and violence, but rather it asks to be guided gently and in such circumstances it can be persuaded to do anything. This, however, must be understood with respect to those who are worthy, and does not apply to those who are evil and wicked or to servile men, who can never be induced to do anything other than by force and by wickedness. For this reason, he says that the latter are not called men, but rather beasts, and because of this they should be treated just like wild, cruel animals, which man masters by blows, starvation and harsh and terrible enclosure.

DC 617

The philosopher Socrates said that the most gracious way there was of administering chastisement was if one were to let one's fury pass in such a way as to speak calmly, and then to take the criminal to task by explaining to him the seriousness of the crime he has committed and the penalty he deserves and what awaits him, and to say all this with a firm resolve and with measured rigour in one's sanction, yet without words of censure. And this ploy is of very great use in keeping a person from berating anyone.

In particular, the person who is chastising must keep from criticising the other for, as Seneca says, the heart of man is noble by nature and is more easily appeased by gentle manners than by force. In *Ecclesiasticus* XIX we read: *Est coertio mendax in ore contumeliosi* (19,28). And it means that constraint is undeservedly present among the words of a person who fulminates, for it should not be there, and nor should any upstanding man recommend constraint to a person prone to vituperation for, in that case, the one who is chastising learns to commit evil more readily. In *Ecclesiasticus* VIII we read: *Ne incendas carbones peccatorum arguens eos* (8,13). And it means that you should not kindle the ire and wickedness of the man whom you are calling to account for, as Tullius says, *De amicitia*,[9] to admonish is the province of true friendship, since it does not leave room for flattery nor, likewise, censure. And Solomon says, *Proverbiorum* XII, that the sensible man must seek to chastise using the greatest restraint and avoiding all blame and anything which might prevent his coercion from being effective in the matter of chastisement or which might provoke his interlocutor to worse. For otherwise the one who is doing the constraining kindles the flames which he should be extinguishing, and kills the person whom he should be reviving and, as a consequence, he remains answerable to God for the harm that he has caused his neighbour on account of his imprudent use of compulsion. In *Proverbiorum* XV we read that *Lingua placabilis lignum vitae; et quo inmoderata est conteret spiritum* (15,4). And it means that soft and gentle language represents life to those to whom one speaks, but speech which is not tempered destroys the whole spirit and entire well-being of the man who listens to it.

TC 870

---

9 Cf. Cicero, *Laelius (De amicitia)*, 88.

3.4. *The dangers of chastising in anger*

A chapter which describes the follies that the said passionate zeal and fervour makes man commit

The first instance of folly in a person whose fervour is injudicious is that often such men cause harm to the innocent and assist those who are guilty for, since they are unable to analyse objectively the actions they perform in such a passionate manner, it follows that, in this way, they are capable of doing harm to the ones as much as to the others. Anticus Cano advises in this respect, therefore, that one should never place a man whose fervour is injudicious in a position of authority. And he attributes the following reason to this, namely that such a man is not able to listen fully to anyone's arguments or to the case for the other side, but rather he will always be satisfied with the first account. [...]

The second case of folly in such men is that they often drive others to despair with their tempestuous outbursts. These men are the ones of whom we read in *Luke* XI: *Si Sathanas Sathanam expellit* (Mt 12,26), that is to say, they wish to cast out the devil from man by acting like the devil himself or, in other words, with unruly fervour; and what they might gently do they do with a stormy temperament. One can apply the words of the Psalmist to these men, namely: *Ignis, grando, nix, glacies, spiritus procellarum, que faciunt verbum eius* (148,8). And it means that the commands of these people are always issued with fire, hail, snow and frost, which betoken wild words and deeds and reveal a tempestuous disposition. They are similar to the man who wished to remove the fly that his lord had upon his forehead with the blow of an axe until he was told to:

"Stop, you madman, stop! It only takes a fan to scare off a fly! An axe is not necessary, for by wishing to kill the fly you shall kill your lord!"

Some people are so imprudent that they wish to impose harsh punishments upon the least mistake, against whom we read in *Ecclesiastes* VII: *Noli esse nimis iustus* (7,17), that is to say, be not overwise nor too ready to judge or punish the crimes of others, though you be a lord, but rather leave some of this to God, and some to His grace and to the free will that God has given to the sinner. And the reason for this is because sometimes you will drive a person to despair if you do not control yourself, for it is written in *Proverbiorum* XXX: *Qui nimis emungit, elicit sanguinem* (30,33). And this means that he who squeezes and milks the breast too forcefully in an effort to extract milk, will end up causing blood to be emitted. And thus he who acts without restraint and overly upsets someone, will eventually make his blood rise, that is to say, will incite him to despair or to another sin or to such straits that, overcome by impatience, he will cause injuries or deaths or some other ills.

We can see from experience that whoever restricts the vapours located in the earth's interior too much so that they cannot escape, causes an earthquake, which often kills men and brings with it many evils. Just as a man overly constrained[10] and upset beyond measure inflicts great harm, and just as a desperate man overcomes all shame and breaks every rule, the chestnut cracks when it burns inside and the heat has no vent within by means of which it might escape. Such is the case when a man is overly constrained, for then there is danger that he will despair and that he will commit some evil. And Joab said to Asahel, *II Regum* II: "Do you not know what an evil thing despair is?" (2 Sam 2,26). Indeed, so evil that it leads men to all kinds of ruin, as is said above. For this reason, Primas Authenticus said that the man who rules must not see nor pay heed to everything he sees, but rather he should feign not to see it when he sees it, and he must overlook many things so that his chastisement has greater efficacy and brings greater advantages in its place.

TC 518

But in addition you may say that your conscience spurs and incites you to do or to say this or that thing. And I say to you that you must consider whether your conscience is not such that it might quite easily make false, rash and fitful judgements, and, for this reason, before you proceed according to the dictates of your conscience, examine whether its promptings are permissible or fanciful, and whether they are appropriate to the time, place and person, and so on for other circumstances. This is why Solomon said, *Ecclesiastes* VII: *Noli iustus esse multum* (7,17). That is to say, do not become over just, for he becomes too just who is not just yet thinks that he is so, deceived as he is by ignorance from knowing what true justice is. And, likewise, he is called over just who, under the pretext or excuse of doing good, and

---

[10] In its archaic sense of being afflicted or distressed. I have retained this term in order to preserve both the literal and the metaphorical senses of the language used by Eiximenis.*

through his ill-judged zeal and remorseful conscience, commits great
follies. And here the *Glossa interlinearis* says the following: *Summum ius
summa est iniustitia. Sunt, enim, qui in nullo volunt condescendere carni et
hoc summa iniustitia est.* And this means that the more that men who
are injudiciously fervent cite their zeal and the cause of justice, the
more they commit injustices and sins, just like those who, due to the
rigour of their ill-judged fervour, do not wish to be compassionate in
any respect towards those who are imperfect or affected by passion,
nor are they able to excuse anything in them. And this is supreme
folly, for God and His vicars, who are wise in many matters, take into
account the needs and the wretched state of those who are imperfect,
for they do what befits their role as beloved fathers who share in the
suffering of their sick children.

As Saint Anthony said, "All things need to be tuned." And he cited
the example of the musical instrument, saying that one could tighten
the strings of a lute so much that they broke and loosen them so much
that they did not make a pleasing sound. One should tune each one
of them, therefore, according to its strength, so that all together they
make a pleasant sound to man. It is thus in the case of our man who
has to rule people, for to cause them too great an affliction drives
them to despair and to give them too free a hand makes rogues and
wicked men of them. For this reason, one must govern with all one's
good sense, for such good sense tunes everything and without that
sense everything is lost. This is why Saint Bernard said: *Non habet cal-
lidus hostis eficacius machinamentum ad tollendam de corde dilectionem quam
si possit facere ut in ea incaute et non rationabiliter ambulet.*[11] And he means
that the devil has no stronger weapons in this world to rid man of love
than that man should fail judiciously to do what he has to do, but that
he should do it in a convoluted manner or one characterised by madness, uproar and shouting and by obstinacy and pride; and, then, that
he should conceal all his folly beneath a zeal for God and should wish
to cover it up, for, in that case, when man thinks he is saving his soul,
then mightily does he damn it. Therefore, when you find yourself at
times inflamed by zeal and before you are stirred to action, remain
calm in your thoughts, while questioning and guiding the said zeal,
impulse or ardour, to see if it is worthy, judicious, permissible and
expedient at that time. And, if it is, put it into practice; and if not,

[11] *Sermones super Cantica canticorum* XIX, 7.

snuff it out from fear of God and for the love of yourself so that you do not fall into madness or sin. And you will find this guidance in *Ecclesiastes* X, which says the following: *Si spiritus potestatem habentis super te ascenderit, locum tuum ne dimiseris, quia curatio cessare faciet peccata maxima* (10,4). And it means that if, at times, you become aware that you are roused by excessive fervour to go too far or to overdo certain things, take care not to be diverted from nor to neglect nor to surpass the limits imposed by God, that is to say, stay within the terms set by your natural reason and your good sense; for reason, when a person follows it, brings an end to great sins which man would commit if he were to follow his unholy fervour, falsely concealed, as this might be, beneath zeal for God. If you doubt whether this zeal is worthy or not, in that case, choose the more certain option, which means that you should not put it into practice until you know for sure that you can do it or that it should justifiably and permissibly be done, while paying heed at all times to the circumstances or, in other words, to the time, place and persons.

TC 521

In whom and why wrath is worse than in others

In olden times, certain spiritual and devout men posed a question, namely that, since anger affected every class of persons, in whom was it worse to be wildly irate. And they received a reply from that great Doctor, Alanus, that it was worst in kings and in sovereigns, for we read in *Proverbiorum* XVI that the wrath of a king is a messenger of death (16,14). [...]

   Second, he said that it was exceptionable in judges also, since wrath is the enemy of the light of truth and extinguishes it. That is why it is very damaging to those who devote themselves to prayer and contemplation as well as to students, according to what Saint Gregory likewise says, in the fifth chapter of his *Moralia*. [...] And Chrysostom mentions, in *Super Johannem, homelia* V, countless evils which follow from this unholy wrath, by reason of which evils he says that it can be compared to fire, to a cruel beast, to a poisonous snake and to rabies and death. And he says that wrath must never arise in the mind of a wise man. And he gives the following reason, namely that if a man is wise, then this unholy wrath has no place in him; but if he is mad, then nobody should feel anger towards him, just as nobody is vexed by children, nor by the blind, the deaf, the mad or the sick. And these are the people who are possessed by fury and mad rage. And he says that just as it cannot be the case that a man should be both healthy and sick at the same time, so also it cannot be the case that a man should be worthy as well as wrathful, for wrath is a sickness of the soul, as we have said above. And he says that, at times and with good reason, upstanding men indeed show anger towards those that they chastise, but they are never truly angry, however, for he says they know that, as the popular saying goes, brief indeed though it may be, anger is a sign of great folly. And this is true, because angry men, just like madmen, do not pay heed to the dangers which might ensue from their rage, nor do they think of the great advantages that they forgo by abandoning patience, nor do they avoid opportunities for their anger, but rather it is clear that they readily seek out all the ills which come of pronounced and uninterrupted wrath. In short, these ills include: loss of good sense; the shortening of their natural life; the poverty of their family; discontentment and death to all those who have to live alongside them; a bad reputation; continual resentment and dissatisfaction, which at times drive them to despair; terrible sin and a bitterness which is reared and ages in the soul, and which causes it to forfeit the good things it achieves when it needs to gain God's grace or glory; in addition to which, it seeks to bring men to a sorry end.

TC 828

3.5. *Three examples*

3.5.1. *Inordinate punishment*

We read of King Samuel of Lycaonia that no one in the world dared to speak ill of any of his own enemies in the presence of this man, for he used to say that to speak ill of one's enemy was to take a womanly and knavish vengeance against him. We read of this same king in the *History of Greece* that his son had an eminent man and prisoner of his killed, and when it was mentioned to his father and he learnt that there was no reason for it, he replied by saying:

"There are three types of scoundrel, that is to say, the peasant scoundrel, who is wicked, because he is a brute animal; then there is the noble scoundrel, who is worse, because he is a vicious wolf; and then there is the royal scoundrel, who is descended from royalty and who, the greater he is the worse he is, because he is a baptised devil, filled with all kinds of evil and completely lacking in shame or fear. And such is my son, whose scoundrel's ways have led him to kill his prisoner. And that is why, from now on, I do not wish him to be called my son nor to receive a share in my legacy, but wish that he bear the name of 'the royal scoundrel'."

And the *History of the East* says in this respect that the son, on hearing that his father had come to loathe him and disinherit him so horribly, said the following:

"Since my father calls me the royal scoundrel and has withdrawn my claim to the kingdom, I promise to God that from now on I shall for ever behave like a right royal scoundrel!"

And it says here that he assembled as many scoundrels as there were in that land and suggested that they tell him which knavish acts he might carry out that were genuinely scandalous. And it says that they advised him to commit the following acts. First, that he should take a whore as his wife and that she should always form part of his council. Second, that he should not show mercy to old women or young, nuns or laywomen, widows or wives, but that he should bring shame upon as many of them as he could. Third, that he should become a notorious robber and should not spare a soul. Fourth, if a lecherous cleric fell into his hands, or this cleric's concubine, he should strip them completely naked and should then shave them from head to toe so that not a hair remained on their bodies which had not been completely shorn. Fifth, that he should not be loyal or true to a soul. Sixth, that he should give himself over to every carnal pleasure and should commit every foul deed that he could without any trace of shame. And they counselled him in various other laws of scoundrelism that are recounted by the *History*, which I do not propose to report for they include very great and hideous acts of villainy which should not be spoken.

So, when he was planning all this in a small town situated near a road, a man named Eusebius, the reverend bishop *tripolitanus*, passed by and was captured by those who were in the company of the said young man. They brought this bishop before him, all shorn and shaven and semi-naked, and he underwent all they did to him with supreme patience. But when he subsequently learnt who this young man was and why he was there and what he had so foolishly planned, the bishop said the following to him:

"My son, your father may call you a scoundrel, but, in truth, you can only be such by reason of your evil deeds. And therefore, do not hold yourself in contempt, my son, nor your soul, and do not cause your enemies to rejoice over you, as God has fitted you to do much good, for which reason do not seek to turn it into evil nor do things which some time soon will bring a horrible death upon your body and a more vile one upon your soul. So, return to your father and humble yourself at his feet, for this is what you must do, and it will be no discredit to you but rather a source of honour, for to do thus is the task of a good son. So, confess your guilt with humility to his face and you shall move him to piety, and shall obtain his mercy and shall return to your former estate."

And it states that this young man realised that the saintly guidance that the said holy bishop had given him was right and, fully edified by his patience and kindly words, he said that he would follow his advice, but he implored him to go first to his father and to appease him, for he was a man who was easily vexed. And the bishop did just this. And when the bishop was with the father he said the following to him:

"My Lord, although, according to what Solomon says, a good father should keep his son close by the rod of correction so that he is good (Prov 13,24), nevertheless the correction must be moderate in order that the son should not give way to despair. For this reason, Saint Paul told parents that they should not aim to cause great indignation in their children, lest they become discouraged (Col 3,21). You," said this bishop, "have caused your son to lose hope. [...] For this reason, I beg you to pardon him this once for the sake of your own honour as well as mine, and he will make satisfaction for his misdeeds as you see fit, and you shall preserve him from despair and your family from shame."

So then the king replied as follows, saying:

"Father, it displeased me greatly that courtesy should not have been shown to my prisoner in my own domains, and that he should not have been shown the kindliness that, in fact, behoves a man who is noble and royal like my son. For this reason, since you have begged me to do this and the arguments you have put forward are so reasonable, I forgive him, but wish him to give satisfaction to the sons of the deceased in such a way that they might be seated at his table at all times, and that he should present them with some notable gift in recompense for the harm done to them as a result of their father's death."

And thus was it done without delay, and the king's son returned to his former estate.

DC 629-630

3.5.2. *The prince who did not know how to blow his nose*

Of this man, in particular, history informs us that he was more dignified in his bearing and more pure in his life than any sovereign who had ever been seen in the East. And history also speaks wonders of his accomplishments, and specifically recounts that they were so many that all kings from the East learnt outright how to live from him and from the tracts that he wrote about the proper comportment of sovereigns, of which rules of comportment I have noted here the following examples.

In the first of these, he stated that a sovereign should show himself to be so fastidious and clean that he was obliged never to do anything which might cause revulsion in anyone. He says on this point, therefore, that when his first-born son once blew his nose in front of everyone using his hand, and immediately afterwards repeated this act using the hood of one of his servants, he reproached him harshly in front of all by saying that he had performed two highly brutish and horrible acts, and that he resembled the son of a vulgar peasant more than that of a king. For to blow one's nose with one's hand is to handle one of the most abhorrent things that exists in this world; which thing is in itself most hideous, but its foulness was doubled when it was carried out in full view of someone, and was then tripled when he used another person's hood to do it, as quite naturally everyone felt great abhorrence at touching such a thing, and all the more so when it belonged to another person. He taught his son on this point, therefore, to move away from others whenever he wished to blow his nose, if he were able to do so, and to turn his face the other way and to blow his nose on his own clothing, without looking at what he had emitted, for he said that to look at such a thing showed that a man was incredibly vulgar and unworthy of any esteem.

DC 777

3.5.3. *The letter that went astray*

The fourth is that the chamberlain should understand that since sovereigns are very haughty, as a rule, and cannot tolerate being chastised by anyone, it is therefore fitting that, when he takes the sovereign to task, he realise that he should do this in the same vein as the doctor who wishes to give bitter pills to the sick man that lacks an appetite in order to induce hunger and health in him. And, therefore, so that the pills do not cause him to vomit, he encloses them within sweet things, such as the yolk of an egg or inverted raisins, in order that the sweetness of the thing, coupled with the bitter pill, might remove all the bitterness of the tablet. Such is the objective then, for the chamberlain must appreciate that being chastised is an extremely hard and very loathsome thing for a sovereign to undergo. And therefore he must fashion the mixture for him with great restraint and without offence to God, and with so much lard and so much honey and sweetness that, even if the sovereign can see it, at least he cannot taste it, so that it does not cause him to be sufficiently disgusted to throw it all back up again and to do worse than he did before.

The said Eliel gives the following example of this, stating that when he wished to reform his sovereign of avarice, first he made out that he was not aware of it in him, but rather that he held him to be the most generous man in the world. And one day he pretended that he had received a letter from a Chaldean friend of his in which the following was said:

> It ill befits you, Don Eliel, that although you have taught your sovereign to perform all kinds of virtuous works, as a result of which he is the most famous sovereign in the East, you have not, however, been able to instruct him in how to be generous and open-handed, which failing, in a sovereign, is one of the most pernicious scourges that there can be in this world. Therefore, I beg you, as one whom I love dearly, without delay to endeavour to make him abandon this vice before he should be defamed any further, so that on this account all his virtues should not be considered unworthy of esteem, nor should he lose the great favours and honours which await him, if the world chose to defame him for this vice.

And the chronicle states that he made sure that this letter went astray, and it came into the possession of the king through other people, just as the chamberlain had arranged. And as a result of this letter, the said sovereign was greatly reformed from his wicked vice of avarice.

He says himself that he used other measures to reform the said sovereign of this vice, by speaking thus:

"My Lord, great must be the honour you show and the blessings you offer to God, Who has granted such exalted honours to yourself and bestowed so many uncommon blessings upon you."

And after he had flattered him, finally he criticised him a touch by saying the following:

"However, my Lord, since I desire your reputation to bear no blemish, I must aver that certain people denigrate you harshly for avarice on account of such and such a thing or such and such a deed. But, in truth, I cannot detect this avarice in you, as things stand; however, in order to do justice to your reputation, you should do this sort of thing and that sort of thing to the contrary."

And he says that by these measures he was able greatly to dissuade him from it. He arranged, likewise, for other people to address similar words to him, and by all these means did they cause him in no uncertain measure to abandon his vice. This Eliel says, however, that the chamberlain must do everything he can to ensure that the sovereign does not think that these reprimands have their origins in him. And this is so that the sovereign does not detest him.

DC 740

4. On how to correct sloth

4.1. *Against drowsy people and perfect sluggards*

Likewise, in fifth place, it is most reprehensible to sleep if the person is sleeping during periods reserved for praying or at times when other people are usually working, for every upstanding man must fall in with the good customs of others so that he is not held to be peculiar nor does he present others with a reason for gossiping, since all peculiarity is loathsome, according to what the Saints say, as well as Scripture, where it is also stated.

It is likewise, in sixth place, most reprehensible to sleep if the person is sleeping on the occasion of someone's preaching or giving a class in the place where he is, or when someone is recounting or proposing something to that person or to others at the same time, for there are certain people who are so brutish that, as a rule, they sleep under such conditions. Of these *Ecclesiasticus* XXII says the following: *Cum dormiente loquitur qui narrat stulto sapientiam* (22,9). And it means that he who speaks, in that case, to those who are asleep in such a manner is just like he who spreads his wisdom over those to whom it is of no avail but who, given that they but rarely ever feel the urge to sleep, are perfectly prepared instead to lapse into slumbers the moment they attend a sermon or lesson. It is certainly a strong sign that anything pertaining to God does not please them. And, therefore, He may utter to them the words of the Psalmist, namely *Surgite postquam sederitis qui manducatis panem doloris* (126,2), that is to say, "Rise up from these your idle slumbers you who eat the bread of sorrow," or in other words, the bread that is wasted on you as on those who do not value wisdom at all or anything that is good.

TC 441

4.2. *Which describes how a person must correct the false prophets of these times*

Besides, their consciences have been blunted and skewed by their wanton intractability, wickedness and obstinacy, for they are as hardened in their wickedness as iron, and incorrigible too. And this is no surprise for, as Solomon says, *Ecclesiastes* VII, nobody can correct whom God has forsaken (7,14). Regarding these and similar people Avicenna offers good advice in his *Metaphysics* when speaking against those who denied the first principle or, in other words, who said that it was not true that each thing either is or is not. He says that one should proceed against such people by means of hard blows until they understand that, when a person strikes someone a blow, then, at such a time, he is not behaving in the same way towards the injured party as if he were not striking him and, as a result, when there are no blows, a person should not say that there are, regarding which situation they maintained the contrary. And once, in England, a warden of the monastery belonging to the Friars Minor in Cambridge was guided by this advice against one of his subordinates, a friar who was headstrong and whimsical, and whose conscience had been blunted, or so the chronicle tells us.

Therefore, you should know that, as the story goes, the said subordinate friar was a student of theology in that very place, and whenever the others went to matins, he put a certain question to himself while lying in his bed, namely whether he should rise for matins or not. And having laid out the arguments on either side, he was of the opinion that those which he had set out on the negative side were stronger and superior, insofar as to consent to the contrary affirmative arguments was highly dangerous and against his conscience. Consequently, he never wished to rise for matins, so swayed was he by his carnal and capricious conscience, which was so skewed and blunted that the bodily love that he bore towards his own person and his slumbers led him to that absurd judgement. However, the afore-mentioned warden, seeing quite how base and shameless the friar was, rebuked him a number of times over why he did not rise for matins in order to praise God along with the others, since he was hale and hearty and young. And that friar always replied that he had qualms of conscience, for, if he were to get out of bed for matins, he would be acting against the judgement of his reason and his conscience. And when the warden had tolerated this for some time, hoping that this friar would mend his ways, and yet saw that the said friar did not wish to be reformed, he said these words:

"My brother, you have qualms of conscience with regard to rising at matins, and I have qualms of conscience because I permit you to do this. Therefore I want you to eat bread and water continually, each day, for as long as you fail to rise for matins."

And he believed that the friar was clearly eating other things in secret, because for this reason he did not wish to get out of bed. So the warden returned to him on the second day, and said to him:

"Brother, why have you not risen for matins?"

And the friar replied, as had become his wont, that he had qualms of conscience. And the warden replied to him that if his scruples were so thoroughgoing, he could eat bread and water from the ground with the cats; and if his conscience were still troubled, he would leave him to make his entry into the town. And so did it go on, on the third day and the fourth, with the friar steadfast in his obstinacy and the warden increasing his penance. And the warden's thoughts passed to the said piece of advice from Avicenna, namely that temerity must be punished by heavy blows, and we read, in addition, that a holy man said: *Hoc genus servorum non nisi cum suppliciis emendatur.* And it means that the type of people who are abject and obstinate can only be made to mend their ways as a result of great beatings. It says, therefore, that the warden then made him attend the chapter, and commanded him to strip completely naked, and he took a great handful of sticks and flogged him harshly, with the result that the skin on his back was riddled with holes and dripping with blood. And when he had disciplined him in this way, the warden asked him the following:

"Tell me, brother, shall you be rising for matins from now on?"

And the friar answered:

"Yes father, willingly!"

And the warden said:

"What will you do about your pangs of conscience then?"

"Father," he said, "it is said that *quia ferrum acuitur ferro*," (Prov 27,17) – which means that iron sharpens iron – "and, therefore, your iron conscience has whetted mine, which was also of iron. And while, at first, my conscience remained lodged in my heart, now, however, it is so keen that it has emerged in its entirety as fumes through the puncture holes that you made with the sticks in my back, and consequently I feel that it shall do me no harm from here on."[12]

Then the warden said to the other friars who were there:

"Brothers, take note of the words that I shall speak to you, and they are these, namely that the best way to break down a capricious conscience is by harsh punishment and penance."

And truly this is how it is, and I even say with full certainty that whosoever were to adhere to this advice against these madmen of our times, who in all their duplicities excuse themselves on grounds of conscience, would find no remedy as reliable as to whip and beat them soundly and to give them harsh and tangible penance, whoever they might be, for they would immediately lay aside their whims of conscience.

SC 63

5. ON HOW TO REFORM FEMININE WICKEDNESS

5.1. *General rules for the schooling of wives*

What approach a man must take towards his wife if he wishes to make a good woman of her

Consequently, on this subject Anticlaudianus described certain very beneficial rules for anyone who might wish to bring his wife to

[12] The Catalan verb 'acuar/agüar', meaning 'to sharpen', has a number of other meanings upon which Eiximenis is playing here, namely 'to punish severely/teach a lesson to' and 'to render a moral or cognitive faculty keener or more acute'.*

order. And the first rule is that a man must never appear to be ignorant to his wife, but rather he should give her to understand that
he knows infinitely more than he seems to, but that what he with-
holds or does not mention, he does so out of love for her, since he
does not wish to grieve or to afflict her and thinks that she will work
it all out little by little.

The second is that a man must never let his wife be overbur-
dened, nor too poor nor too rich, and neither should he entrust
her with his money, for excesses such as these will make her depart
from the rules.

The third is that, in the beginning, no husband should grant his
wife all possible freedoms, for, if he later opts to impose restrictions
upon her, he shall always find her disquieted. Consequently, it is better if he can continually extend her liberty, and every small concession
he makes to her she will take to be a major favour.

The fourth is that a man must always show great discretion towards
his wife so that she judges him to be a noble man and a man of truth
and great superiority, and he should not be mean or deceitful towards
her nor reveal any noteworthy vice; for, if he does, she shall despise
him with a vengeance and shall never serve him willingly, and, if she
sees the contrary of that vice in another man, she shall love that man
with all her heart. In spite of this, however, a man can give his wife to
understand that he possesses a great vice, a vice on account of which
women do not disdain a man but fear him all the more. And the vice
in question is a diabolical fury so potent that, the day that it takes him,
he would forgive neither his father or mother but would stab and kill
everyone, if there were cause for it.

The fifth is that a man must pay heed to his wife's natural condition, that is to say, to whether she has good sense or is of unsound
mind or capricious. If she has good sense, a man can reform her of
her vices by using fine and gentle words. If she is capricious, she will
need to be straightened out by harsh measures. And he must take
note also of whether she is humble or proud for, if she is proud and
he shows her great love, her head will swell; and all the more so if,
by her nature and particular desires, and on the advice of old
women, she wishes to dominate her husband. For then the husband
can consider himself to be a captive and to be tormented, for Holy
Scripture states that *Mulier, cum primatum habet, contraria est viro* (Eccl
25,30). And it means that when a woman has ascendancy over her

husband she is always at odds with him in everything; and such women make it a rule that within three years, come what may, they shall have subdued their husbands in whatever way they can, and, as soon as a man has had the misfortune to fall captive to her but once, he can consider himself to be tormented for ever more.

The sixth rule is that a man must know how to use discretion in speaking to her regarding what displeases him and in chastising her for her faults, for almost all of man's affairs – on any subject which he has to handle using words – consist of his being able to put language to good use. For if he does this, he can quite easily censure his wife in such a manner that it seems that he is saying these things out of great love, or that he does not utter his words out of hatred, but rather that it displeases him that he has to say them, or that certain people say these things but that he excuses her of them. And by such means and similar can a man set forth his affairs.

The seventh is that a man must consider the place where he says these things to her, for he must not say them to her in front of other people nor in a place which might put her to shame, but to one side, with the greatest indications of love that he is able to convey in words.

DC 539

On how the faults of the female sex can provide subject matter for teaching women to behave well

Once he has paid heed to all the said rules, a man can formulate many lessons and reprimands with regard to each of the said failings and natural and moral virtues that women may possess. And, to start with, by attending to the first virtue, namely her sense of modesty, you must do all that you can to ensure that you make it flourish in her by praising such modesty and women who possess it, and by saying how you love her for her modesty and because she is renowned for being reserved, and that whoever is reserved possesses every favour, for of what value is a woman who lacks a sense of shame? And you can say the following to her: "Oh what great displeasure it causes me to see that woman behaving so shamelessly!" Second, on account of her passive nature and fittingly timorous qualities you can master her, bring her to order and cause her to do whatever you wish. Consequently, on account of these two virtues they possess, namely shame and fear, you can reform them of their wicked passions and of their faults, you can inspire them to do

all kinds of good, and you can set them right by yourself. And at times
it is better that you let some honourable matron do this to whom she
gives credence.

The *Historia Romana* describes how King Grisantus of Mesopotamia
had five wives, who were the most troublesome in the world, and he
set them straight in this manner. He could count upon honourable
women who, whilst they were with them, pretended that they took
their side so that they might take them to task better, but secretly the
king had already informed them what they were to say and do, and
those matrons always instructed them in such a way as to make them
do what the king wished. And these matrons themselves had secret
talks all alone with the king concerning everything that they had said
and done, and what they were to say and do with them, and what they
knew about them. And with what the king told them and what the
women were able to add to this, in the end they achieved everything
they wanted.

And it states here that the king informed them of the following
things in particular: first, to love their husbands and to honour their
in-laws, and to behave themselves and run their households as best
they could. He instructed them also to observe chastity, by telling them
that nature could not bring it about that a bastard child might possess
what belonged to a man of whom he was no kin, and that the true
heirs be dispossessed. And this is what married women do who are not
chaste. And thus the matrons placed shame and fear before them, for
by reason of each of these fine qualities in women must they strive to
be chaste, for a base woman brings shame upon herself and her entire
kind – better she were dead; she brings shame upon her husband and
her children, and she betrays the loyalty she promised to her husband
in matrimony. And therefore, by frequently carrying out such acts, she
then lets herself be carried away by a passion so powerful that, subsequently, she is unable to renounce it, and the men to whom such
women consent a little or a great deal go on to congratulate themselves and make mountains out of molehills. And this evil does away
with the good sense of learned men, and of women all the more, who
have less of it! And therefore not only must honourable women abhor
such a thing in another woman, as well as showing their husbands that
it disgusts them, but the obligations of matrimony impel them to do
so. And for this reason, they instructed them well in matters of eating
and drinking, by telling them that overeating and -drinking often

leads women to fall into the sin of lust – the Romans, therefore, rarely drank wine – and how one of the most repulsive things in the world is a woman who fornicates or is drunken, to which effect Solomon says that such a woman is more loathsome than the dung which lies in the street (Ecclesiasticus 9,10). And consequently, they can be made to abandon their excessive talking, for the woman who remains silent is more agreeable to her husband and shows that she has good sense, and that she knows the meaning of virtue and honour, and reveals that she is of high birth, and for this reason she enjoys an excellent reputation. And the woman who hears that such things can be said of her, remains silent and does all she can in order that she might be praised. Likewise, by these means you can prevail upon her to be steadfast and faithful, for her husband will give greater credence to her. And the same applies if their behaviour is not capricious, nor do they look conceitedly back and forth, but are fully composed and modest, with the result that the one thing bears witness to the other, in such a way that the public cannot learn of any bad reputation nor the husband have reason for suspicion.

DC 540

5.2. *Wives must submit to their husbands*

On how women revert to their wickedness if one lets them have ascendancy

What we have discussed above also seems true, namely that to a large extent women may revert to their wickedness if one lets them have ascendancy, for we read in *Ecclesiasticus* XXV, *Mulier si primatum habeat, contraria est viro suo* (25,30). And it means that, if a woman enjoys dominance over her husband in the home, then she will not hesitate to be at odds with him at all times. And the reason for this is that the condition and estate in which God has created woman is that she should be subordinate to her husband. And the blessed Lord said precisely this to the first woman after she had sinned, using the words, *Sub potestate viri eris* (Gen 3,16). And He meant that women would be under their husbands' power. And in order to indicate this subordination, women in Tartary wear upon their heads the form of a foot, which serves to adorn their heads, just as, among us, exalted women adorn their heads with crowns or garlands. So, therefore, by divine order, by the law of nature and by general and approved custom, women should be subordinate to their husbands, and if men were to let women have ascendancy over them, it would be only fitting that the first people they attacked as a result of this ascendancy should be men. It is written, *Proverbiorum* XXIX, that *Qui delicate nutrit servum suum, inveniet contumacem* (29,21). And this means, in short, that he who treats the one who must serve him too indulgently, shall meet great rebellion where he should meet humility, subordination and obedience to his person. And do not think that this rebellion and wickedness which women practise against their husbands in such a case is but a small thing, for rather it is so great and so terrible that without hesitation such a woman will have the audacity to inflict great disgrace upon her husband in the sight of the entire world and to treat him just like a manservant. [...]

I met a noble knight in Catalonia who, in his old age, took a wife of common birth so that he might be treated better. And his wife, who found that she occupied a very high station on account of her husband, began to quarrel with him and to show contempt towards him. And in order to reduce her pride and wickedness, as soon as her husband saw her lose her senses, he instructed one of his squires to issue a sound and full reproach to her in front of him, wishing to give her to understand that she was not worthy of being touched by him in person. And she, seeing how great was her loss of prestige, reformed herself of her madness. Or, if she did not wish to be brought to order by the said means, he would take the keys away from her and prevent her from running the household and would entrust it to a woman whom his wife could not stand, this other woman being under instructions not to give her a loaf of bread without the master's permission. And consequently, being subject to the continual application of such methods, and worse, at times she lost her audacity and returned to her senses. [...]

Moreover, for this reason, it is also not good for a woman to be allowed to have ascendancy, for if it is then taken away from her, her wickedness grows beyond measure for, afterwards, she considers as her right what you granted her as a favour, and takes mortal offence if she is deprived of it, even if only for an hour. Furthermore, it must likewise not be allowed her because when a woman takes something for granted, her inappreciativeness is a truly horrible thing for, whatever great advantages she may have received, she immediately refuses to acknowledge both God and everything that has been given to her. This is because the vapours from the vanity they possess and from their pleasure at the great honour that has been done them, immediately absorb that small degree of sense they have and, therefore, they show no gratitude at such times and fail to recall the advantages they have received.

Consequently, in order to avoid this, you must know that a distinguished man from Catalonia took a mere girl for his wife, of common birth, so that he might better be served by her. And you must know that, when he married her, the said man of quality took all of the miserable and wretched clothes that the said girl wore before she was his wife, and he kept them locked up in a chest in his bedroom. And the methods he applied to her were as follows: for as soon as she began to lose her head, he made her take off the decent clothes she was wearing and dress up in the torn and tattered ones that she had worn before she was his wife. And he wished her to wear them until she had regained her composure, and she, seeing how very great was her loss of prestige, took great care not to lose her wits. Therefore her husband said to her at times:

"My lady, whatever the gamewarden might say, it is fear that protects the vineyard."

TC 96

By what means a man can deflate the wickedness, audacity or arrogance of his wife

Once a philosopher asked another philosopher, named Belligerus, what methods a man can use on a woman so that she does not dominate the man. And Belligerus replied in the following words:

"If a man desires what you say, he must pay heed to whether the woman is spirited and domineering in her nature or not. If she is not, it is not necessary to employ as harsh a manner or style as the following, but rather a man can calm her in the way that seems best to him. In the event, however, that she is particularly spirited, haughty and dominant, the man should, at first, show her that he is a man of good morals and a lover of truth above all things, and that he is trustworthy, wise, discreet and secretive, and that he does not reveal his thoughts to anyone at all. Also, he should let her know that he is someone who has all due respect for propriety, but not so much that, should the circumstances require it, he would be incapable of acting with force. And these two things generate fear and reverence for man in a woman's mind.

"Also, he must make it clear to her that a man desires to be well-served by a woman or by any other in all matters which pertain to him, and that he will not tolerate the slightest divergence from this requirement. Furthermore," this philosopher said, "he must treat her in this fashion, namely he should never ask for her guidance on any subject, however much good sense she has, or if he does, he should then pretend that he does not mean to speak to her about those matters of which he tells her in order to elicit her advice, but that it is a question of chance that he has said these things. And, in the event that she goes on to give him good advice, this man should pretend to attach little importance to it when all is said and done. And, if he must do as she has advised, the man should attribute it to another in her presence, saying that this very man had already offered that piece of advice, and that the others, who had approved of it, wish things to be done in that manner, just so that she does not think that something is being done on the basis of her advice. And when she speaks extremely good sense, then, out of contempt, he should move away from her while jeering loudly or laughing, and say, 'All women are mad!' or 'You don't know what you are saying!', so that she does not boast of being able to give advice, for that would make her head swell, and for that reason she would have the audacity to think that her husband could not do anything without her guidance."

TC 97

5.3. On how one can reform the wickedness of women by means of fear

This same philosopher states, furthermore, the following noteworthy doctrine, namely that in order to save women from wickedness it is best to keep them in a state of fear and to not let them have ascendancy. Keeping them in a state of fear, when that fear is mild, prevents them from saying and doing evil things and from revealing wickedness, for a woman's dread should arise from love and her sense of modesty rather than from apprehension of injury. Housemaids should be fearful of injury, yet it is very harmful for a wife to have to mend her wicked ways from dread of injury. And it is a mark of great nobility in her that she should always be in fear of her husband, though not an abject fear that dreads beatings alone; instead, her fear must be that of a friend, born from love and reverence, just like the dread of him who only fears the other inasmuch as he would not want to give offence to him, so that he might not lose his love or offend his honour, which he wants and desires.

It is true that sometimes you will encounter women so shameless, wicked and unreasonable that they fear no one at all unless they dread the stick and fear that they shall be handled roughly and injured, as a result of which there are some who are not prepared to do what they should for any other reason. But I shall tell you now about a terrible thing, for know that there are women who, even so, cannot resist being hurt, and so much so that, if they find that their husbands do not beat them, they employ special ruses to provoke the latter into assaulting them. I can tell you about one, in particular, who was like this; for, although she was chaste, nevertheless when she realised that her husband did not wish to injure her for any other act of wickedness that she might commit towards him or words that she might address to him, one day she knowingly left the stopper off the wine vessel in his presence so that he would harm her over the spilling of the wine. And when she realised that she still could not provoke him into hurting her, she was on the point of going out of her mind. And consequently, when matters are such that they desire ill-treatment with a vengeance, by my faith should they have it and in such a manner that their very urge to receive it should disappear completely; always observing restraint, however, and by a more decent means than this, if it can be achieved, for one can employ such means that it is far better to inspire in them a fear which is seemly than to hurt them with all one's might. [...]

When Veteranus, the philosopher, was asked by what means one could recognise a wise man if that man did not have important affairs through which he might manifest his wisdom, he replied that it was by his ability to calm a woman down when she was upset. When asked of what this ability to produce such a calming effect consisted, he replied that it lay in one's being able prudently to impose upon her mind a sense of fear mingled with love, as well as a propensity to feel reverence towards those to whom she should. And, to this end, it is necessary for the man to come across to the woman as a person who possesses good sense, and is truthful and honourable, for, if the woman does not hold the man in any esteem, insofar as she considers him to have a certain goodness and nobility about his manners, she shall never love him completely nor shall she willingly obey him.

What we intended to prove is clear, therefore, namely that the wickedness of women can be reformed by means of fear and dread.

TC 95

III

1. The sovereign's books

1.1. *Which details those books which are necessary to a sovereign*

Celidonius teaches in his *Rules* which books are necessary to a sovereign; and he says that, first of all, he requires a book giving information upon God's law, with regard to which a man of the Church should instruct him. And Our Lord specifically gave this command to the people of Israel, *Deuteronomii* XVII, using these words: "After your king has been raised to the throne and crowned, he shall have the book of my law with him, from which the priests will inform him about the law" (Deut 17,18-19). And we read *libro quinto Ecclesiasticae Historiae* that Ptolemy, king of Egypt, had the seventy interpreters of the Bible come to him so that he might know God's law. And David kept the prophet, Nathan, and the priest, Zadok, with him, to instruct him about the law.

And we read about the great Emperor Theodosius in the prologue to the *Historia tripartita*[1] that by day he concerned himself with matters relating to the governance of the empire, but that only by night, after he had retired, he undertook to study divine matters and to consider those things that he had to do by day, for it is written that night must assist day just as the servant his master. Sovereigns, then, must know God's law better than anyone, as well as those things which we must believe, what we must expect, what we must dread, what we must shrink from and avoid and what we must say and do. And it is

---

[1] Cf. Cassiodorus Vivarensis, *Historia tripartita* (PL 69, col. 882 C).

not only the books of the law which assist us in knowing these things, but also various other books which are written about vices and virtues and about the governance of sovereigns. Moreover, he must have only those books which may be of advantage to him with regard to the said matters, and he must also have books which teach him how to give counsel and how to fight battles, and which teach him about matters pertaining to his office. And this writer said, in particular, that likewise he must have books for praying, and, in this respect, have prayers for different requirements and different times, such as those for praying at matins and at vespers, and those for Mass. And take care not to hold nor to touch the missal, out of reverence for the Holy Sacrament of the altar, for, as the Holy Patriarch Arcadius of Alexandria said, this book should only be touched by a priest. [...]

According to what is stated in the *History of the East*, Orpheus, king of Havilah, said that in every king's or sovereign's residence there should be a study or place so designed that the sovereign might study there, and the sovereign should enter this place every day in order to read some good things at least which might offer him guidance in the affairs with which he had to deal. For he said that the best and the most trustworthy counsellors of all were good books and that the human race, in particular, should always offer great thanks to God, Who had enlightened, instructed and consoled it on all subjects by means of so many fine books. And he said that a sovereign without books and without a study was not worthy of being a sovereign, for he lacked half or almost all of the learning that he needed. The *History* narrates in this respect that Geron, a vigorous old man, who was cho-sen to be king in Laxie, in the High Indies,[2] said:

"I shall never reign or pass judgement until I am able to read."

And within five months he was able to read, and he always read at night for the duration of two candles. And, consequently, nobody dared speak to him at night, so he said these words to his people:

"Since I devote all my days to you, leave the nights to me, for what I do each night redounds to your favour."

DC 501

[2] Cat. *Laxsia*; presumably the city of Laxie or Li-hsieh (29° 43' 54" North 121° 36' 50" East) in eastern China.*

1.2. *Why a sovereign should not be a tyrant and what tyranny is*

Aristotle, in the fifth book of his *Politics*,[3] describes the many differences between a good king and a tyrant, which we shall state here along with others which have been mentioned by the Doctors. The first is that a king is always concerned with the good and with the good of the community, but the tyrant is always concerned with his own good. The second is that the king, since he devotes himself to the good of the community, as has been stated, consequently attends to a good which is honourable and worthy of esteem; but the tyrant, since he is committed to his own pleasure, and principally to the pleasures of the flesh, always gives his mind to things for which he deserves every dishonour, ignominy and shame. [...]

The fourteenth is that, while kings, in their kingdoms, promote the study of various sciences and show favour to men of great learning so as better to instruct their people and to receive guidance in good governance from them, tyrants, on the other hand, persecute these men of wisdom and learning so much that they do not leave one of them alive. And they do this because, their lordship being contrary to reason and to justice, they fear, therefore, that if they were to have knowledgeable men in their territories, such men would teach the people to oppose tyrants and the populace would rebel or kill them or eject them from their domains, just as, on the contrary, these same learned men persuade the people to love and honour good kings, by making them realise and appreciate the good things that they have done for their kingdoms. [...]

In his *Politics*, Aristotle reduces all the said wiles to four. And they are these: the first is that tyrants do their best to ensure that their subjects are coarse and ignorant, so that they are not able to find a way of attacking them; the second is that their subjects be terrified, so that no one dares to rise up against them; the third is that their subjects be poor, so that there are not sufficient to wage a war against them; and the fourth is that they should not band together, so that they are unable to attempt anything against him.

DC 602

3 Cf. *Politics* VI, 11

2. THE STUDIES OF CITIZENS

2.1. *Which teaches those things that every citizen must know depending on the estate to which he belongs*

According to the *Bulgarian Chronicle*, when Polimarchus Calcedonensis, the jurist and distinguished philosopher, was asked with which things in particular the citizenry should be acquainted, he replied that, generally speaking, they should all know how to speak and to behave courteously, for it is the concern of every citizen to be civil and tactful. And each person should know a certain amount about soldiery, according to his estate, and should refrain from those foul crimes which deprive a man of his reputation in every respect.

He also said that, since a city is divided between those of lower, middle and higher rank, therefore those of lower standing should each know their trade to the best of their ability and should have dealings with those who travel outside their country, such as merchants, so that they can note whether the practitioners of their particular trade in the lands visited by these merchants make use therein of some subtlety or particular skill with which they might be unfamiliar, in order that they might learn it and put it into practice. Those of median and higher rank should know Latin grammar in order to be able to converse with foreigners within their own country and outside of it. Those of the highest rank must know about the country's laws, constitutions, councils and customs, and must have experience as councillors, and must have special books on these subjects, detailing how our forefathers governed, what the experience of our current rulers is, the reputations of those who live far away, the practices of those who live close by and of those who have been the best and most sensible rulers.

For this reason, Saint Jerome states in his prologue to the *Bible* that the great men of old who took care of the governance of communities all around the world always pursued knowledge. And he gives countless examples of this in the same work, for he says that there is as huge a difference between a knowledgeable and an ignorant man as there is between light and dark and that holy rustics and peasants are only able to be of profit to themselves, whereas a wise and knowledgeable man is just like the helsman of a ship who, by his skilful handling and direction, saves himself and all the others. Rome, therefore, always afforded supreme reverence to the Senate, namely, its multitude of councillors, endowing them with great honours, great privileges and great riches, for they said that these men were the fathers of the city, the mothers of the people, the life of the community, the exaltation of the state, the crown of the empire, the eyes of the world, the light of the laws, the succour of the wretched, the weapons of the nobility, and patrons of all that pertained to the common people. On account of this in particular, therefore, Cato, in death, informed his son that he should always devote himself to the study of fine books, of important words of counsel and of famous teachings, for he said:

"Since I leave you sufficient wealth for you to live, according to your station, without having to work, do not sully yourself with the horrid offence of avarice which renders you ignoble and discredits you in the eyes of God and the world, as well as preventing you from performing noble acts and applying yourself to profitable knowledge and to learning. For foolish is the man who, if he can live comfortably according to his station, would for any extra amount of money set aside the study of wisdom, through which study he deserves to be pleasing to God and to exercise authority in the world, as well as to govern himself and to be honoured and loved by every creature."

Solomon said, therefore, *Proverbiorum* XVII, that *Quid prodest stulto habere divitias, cum sapientiam emere non possit?* (17,16). And it means this, namely what does it avail a fool to win or to earn riches given that he knows that one cannot use one's wealth to buy wisdom nor any profitable knowledge, both of which are things that a man must desire more than anything else in the world except God? The reason, according to what Saint Gregory states in his *Morals*, is because a man who possesses wisdom has God, the world and himself, and without it he is a great brute unworthy of living among men.

We read of Plato the Great that, when he was on the point of dying, he had all of his books brought to him, and he kissed and embraced them all, and gave instructions that they should always be held in great reverence. And he spoke as follows to these said books of his:

"Revered and magisterial parents of mine, lights of my life, from here on I can no longer be with you, for I am departing for my God, who calls me this very instant. I offer you that gratitude with which I am familiar and of which I am capable for the great honour, reward and glory that you have given me in this world, and I beseech my Lord and God to put you into the hands of people who shall always value, honour and seek you out with all their hearts, just as I have done throughout my life."

And then, having done this, it says that he turned to his followers and said to them:

"My dear sons, may these be the last words that, from now on, you ever have to hear from me, namely that you should value wisdom and profitable knowledge after God, and that for the sake of wisdom you should not spare money in order to acquire worthy teachers or good books, for both of these things are priceless, insofar as they make a man out of the one who values them, and within these two things is enclosed all the treasure, wealth and nobility of this world."

DC 14

2.2. *From which books a nobleman and a good citizen should study*

In olden times certain philosophers in Rome posed and discussed the question of what a noble citizen should know, as well as what he should study and with regard to what, in particular, he should display his knowledge and wisdom, and finally they decided thus. And, first of all, they replied, in connection with their first query, that every worthy and respectable citizen, and all the more so every prominent figure, such as a knight, a nobleman, a duke or a sovereign, must and should know the languages which are spoken in the surrounding countries, and also they must learn Latin grammar in order to be able to understand the useful books that are written in Latin, and so as to be able to converse with foreigners should these be learned and so that they might be able to reason with them without an interpreter.

Also they must have to hand certain worthy and celebrated books concerning morals, such as the famous histories written by the ancients which have met with approval, and especially the *Books of Kings* which are in the *Bible*, and the creation of the world in the book of *Genesis*, and the five other books which follow, called the *Books of Laws*, and the *Book of Judges*, which comes after them, and that of Maccabees and all the other famous books and historical accounts and the like which are within the *Bible* as well as outside it. Also they should be familiar with the books of wisdom which are in the *Bible*, for these are very moral, and also the holy Gospels, for these contain parables and lofty Christian wisdom and they soften one's heart with the love of the Saviour.

Also, they must be able to give guidance and know how to speak eloquently upon any subject which might be required of them, as is taught by the *Rhetorics* of Aristotle and Tullius and of various others who have spoken on this matter. In addition, they must be acquainted with some of the great philosophers who have discussed the governance of the people, soldiery and political life, such as Vegetius in his *De re militari*, and Valerius Maximus, and Titus Livius, Trogus Pompeius, and Boethius in his *De consolatione* and *De scholastica disciplina*, and Hugh in his *Didascalicon*, and the *Summa collationum* and various other short works written by Brother John of Wales, from the order of the Friars Minor. And it would be useful, also, if they were to be acquainted with the solar system and knew something about astrology in order to take advantage of these things in many cases which are subject to chance or to natural contingencies. And it falls, in particular, to the lot of distinguished people to have special books concerning matters of conscience, such as the *Book of vices and virtues* and those which treat of eternal torment and of the glory of paradise, in order to live virtuous lives, for all things in the present life ultimately have their end in the latter, just as has been discussed above.

Everything that has been said to apply to good citizens, applies much more to knights and noblemen and all the more so to those of higher standing, for the more distinguished a person is, the more it behoves him to know and desire to a greater degree those things which render him virtuous and noble, in the same way that it is stated above that nobility, strictly speaking, is based more upon the excellence of one's morals and of the virtuousness of one's life than upon one's being of high birth and descending from a noble family.

DC 192

2.3. *Reading as an antidote to the perils of idleness*

The fourth [rule] is that the good citizen must concern himself in his home with virtuous and agreeable things which prevent him from becoming vexed there. And this is the case because whoever flees from crowds must remain in his house, whereby he must occupy his mind with pleasant things which keep him at home and which teach him to do what he has to do when he is among other people. These pleasant things include lofty thoughts concerning heavenly matters and virtuous topics and the affairs of the community as well as those of his own;

and also the study of noble books, which assist him in carrying out his business and, for this reason, he must avoid all study which is not profitable or is harmful like the plague. And, furthermore, he may honourably apply himself to playing decorous instruments, and to transforming that pleasure into the glory of God, or he may devote himself to manual tasks within his home or he may conduct discussions, in confidence, with some agreeable and upstanding person. [...]

The sixth is that, for all that the good citizen must remain at home a great deal in order to avoid the presence of crowds, he must nevertheless ensure that neither the community nor others should forfeit anything as a result of his remaining at home so long, and that by his remaining indoors he does not vex his wife or the maidservants. For this very reason, the distinguished citizens of Rome had large and spacious houses, so that while they were in one part of their lodgings, their wives could work as they pleased in the other. Furthermore, so that they could take flight from crowds they had beautiful orchards or sizeable farmsteads, in which they often took recreation and which they likewise did so as not to cause annoyance to their wives or to their servants.

DC 83

3. THE STUDIES OF A KNIGHT

3.1. *General guidance*

Which continues the subject by also teaching loyal knights how they should live

Lycurgus, the great sovereign and jurist from Greece, ordered knights to live in their castles, outside the cities, so that there they might devote themselves more readily to the study of noble books and to a virtuous life. He also did this in order that they might be seen less frequently by those who dwelt in the cities, so that they might be held in higher esteem and met with greater eagerness when they passed among them; and also so that they might hear less about the delights of the city and might be strong, wise people, full of every virtue instead of being self-indulgent. And he ordered that a man of high birth who was dissolute in his manner of living or a companion to rogues or whose talk or conversation was foul, or who was badly brought up or inobedient to his father or mother, or who was tainted by any vice, could never be a knight, but should be stripped of his nobility instead and placed among the peasants as if he were of low birth and shunned for all time.

LA III, 59

3.2. The decadence of the knightly class on account of their failure to study

Which describes other wise recommendations of that same Duke

My son, always be eager to study wisdom, for this pertains supremely to a nobleman. And know this, my son, that in olden times nobles alone were learned men and judges. And do you think that the Roman régime allowed the sons of peasants and of common people to judge themselves or to judge cities and towns? Certainly not, but see, my son, what the foolishness of noblemen has done, that has forsaken the study of wisdom, which was their chief glory, and has chosen the least part, namely devotion to violence and to the particular profession of soldiery; and, therefore, God punishes them most hideously for this sin, for today the sons of peasants throughout the world have taken command of the study of wisdom that the nobles have forsaken and they stand in judgement over these nobles and have taken their chief honours, since these nobles have to be judged by them. And further, they have taken all their privileges, for the nobles go to perform feats of arms and these people sleep in their homes in the cities and large towns. And what's more, they have taken their profits, for a learned man is immediately wealthy and a nobleman almost never or rarely; and, moreover, the learned man can pick up as much money as he likes from attending a meeting or from giving counsel, while a knight may remain on the field of battle against the enemy night and day, all for a florin, and risks losing his life and his possessions. See then, my son, what their disdain for wisdom has done! I beg you, then, always to seek it, to desire it, to value it and to study it, for it shall be as a great crown upon your head and shall give great glory to your family.

My son, do not forsake nobility for any reason nor the noble manners of eminent men and do not place your faith in the nobles who are in the world today, for all nobility is now forgotten, for they know nothing about it. But seek to emulate the nobility of which you read in your books regarding the great men of old and you shall see, if you compare their deeds with those of the present, that any distinction that exists in the world today is something very vile and very gross and a great insult to the origins from which they are descended. The philosopher Orpheus, therefore, advised all the southern kings henceforth not to make any knights from the descendents of the knights of old, because all of these had lost every sign of distinction and high birth, and he advised them to make new knights, who should all be made so in the old manner, that is to say, through the selection of a thousand men.

DC 889

4. THE STUDIES OF WOMEN

4.1. *The shortcomings of women*

On how the wickedness of a woman is greater than any other wickedness, and for what reasons

When the philosopher Ecciduus was asked in whom is found the greatest wickedness and the least good sense, he replied that it is found in women, and this agrees with what we read in *Ecclesiasticus, capitulo* XXV, which states that *Non est malitia super malitiam mulieris* (25,17). And it means that there is no greater wickedness than the wickedness of a woman. And the said philosopher attributes the following reasons to this.

The first is that women are easily stirred, for he says: *Quid est mulier nisi mollis aer?* or, in other words: "What is woman but a gentle breath of air?", for thus are they stirred without warning just like the air. And this is the reason why they immediately believe what they hear. And, therefore, a woman has to be good for her not to wish to hear a great deal from people other than those to whom she is obliged to listen, such as her father or husband or brother or people who have been judged to be worthy, for if she wishes to listen to whomsoever she pleases, doubtless she will cause herself a lot of trouble. Even so, however, just as a breath of air is quickened all of a sudden, so a woman is soon stirred if an opportunity presents itself to her or if she herself takes it, as in fact often happens.

The second reason is because, by nature, women have little sense and, as a result, they do not have sufficient restraints upon their wickedness. The third is that, in general, coldness and phlegm prevail in women, and when cold things are heated up they are incomparably more fiery than any others. So, when their fury is thus inflamed, this high degree of fieriness upsets at once the little understanding they have and they become mad in almost every respect when they are irate. But note here that, for all that women are by nature cold, and for this reason should become inflamed with great difficulty, the urges they feel when they lose their temper are so sudden and so pronounced, that the violent impulse that pulls her along is far more powerful than the cold matter from which her nature is formed.

The fourth is that, by nature, they are difficult to handle for the reasons stated in the *Eighth* book, where we spoke about the physical form of women, and the form of their body bears witness to this, for they are stout below and slender above. And the body of a well-built man ought to be the opposite of this, namely, slender from the chest down and broad in the chest and shoulders, with a short, thick neck, and his head likewise; the opposite of which is found in women. And it is very clear that this is in their nature, for when they are in their mother's womb they show opposite signs to the males and bring on revolting urges in pregnant mothers, such as that of wishing to eat soil or to nibble at stones and coals. And when they are born the first thing they say is 'e', which is a bad-tempered and back-to-front letter. It is clearly bad-tempered because, in general, when somebody wishes to fight another, that person will first of all confront him with a cry of "'e(e)!" as in "'Ee, Mister!", etc. It is back-to-front, moreover, since it turns its back in every respect upon the letter 'a', which is the first letter that a man says when he is born. As a result, these letters have conceived an enmity for each other and, on the contrary, turn their backs on each other, thus suggesting that men and women, who are the first to utter them, are looking at each other the wrong way round at moments when they lose affection for each other. And the letters 'b' and 'c', which come between 'a' and 'e' in the alphabet, suggest the same, for 'b' and 'c' can never be united or conjoined with any letter. And thus there can never be true harmony between men and contrary women until the full cause of their disturbance is removed.[4]

And this philosopher recommends, therefore, that when a man sees a woman horribly moved to anger, that woman will never pass into madness nor fall into great wickedness if he goes along with what she says and speaks gently to her, and this approach is highly effective;

4 Beyond Eiximenis', to the modern reader's eye, rather obscure analogical references to letters of the alphabet, he is interweaving in this paragraph the literal and the figurative senses of the adjective *revés/-essa*, meaning, literally, back to front or the wrong way round and, figuratively, hard to handle, unruly, contrary, and even revolting.*

and, subsequently, when the woman has fully come to her senses, the man can then say to her what he wishes. And, if it is the case that the man wishes to prevent her from falling into such a state of capricious wickedness and of contrariness, he must always give her a preamble which will soften her heart, such as telling her that he loves her this much and that much and that he intends always to maintain the same love for her if she desires it, but that she should do this thing and that thing, on account of which things she would be worthy of this reward and that. And thus, finally, he can move on to real words and harsh and stern deeds according to the nature of the fault she has committed. But, if you fly at her in a rage, you will make her lose her senses, as a result of which, if she is completely overcome by anger, there is no disaster in this world that she will not bring upon you and herself. And this is true insofar as one often sees that they are so overtaken by wickedness that it causes the natural love they bear in their hearts to perish, to such a degree that they will not hesitate to kill their husbands and their children. And it is also true that, if they are able to do as they wish, they will have no fear of bringing death or any kind of foul thing in this world upon themselves.

Therefore my lord Saint Peter reminded men, in his *First Epistle*, *capitulo* III (7), to support their wives just like fragile vessels of glass, for God has made them in this way. And one must consider that, although God has made them in this way, He has also made them, however, so that they might always have glory with Him in paradise. And one must consider that, however noble and rich they might be, the anguish, affliction and hardship that they undergo are great, as are the services they perform for men. And, because of these things, one must graciously endure them, for, beyond what has been said, man acquires great merit in doing so during this present life and by it one does great service to God. And, besides, one is very much obliged to do this on account of the singular service that every class and rank of man throughout the world receives from them at all times.

TC 93

4.2. *The schooling of girls*

How girls should be raised

Now let us see what kind of education is the lot of girls and maidens. And in this respect you will note, first, that, according to what Tullius

117

states in his *De officiis*, girls and maidens are of different ages, for she is usually called a girl who is between ten and twelve years old, and from twelve until the age when a woman has a husband she is called a maiden. And he says that the age for a maiden to marry begins at eighteen and lasts until she is twenty-five, and from then on her time for marrying has passed. And in keeping with this difference of ages, he mentions various customs which must be taught both to the ones and the others.

And on this subject Carnotensis says, first of all, in his book called *De moribus sacris* that, as soon as a girl has use of her reason and a certain amount of good sense, one must give her instruction on things that regard God, such as that she might know how to cross herself, and say the Our Father and the Hail Mary and the *Credo in Deum*, and that she might know to kneel before the images of Jesus Christ and the Holy Virgin Mary; and that, if she hears someone say "Blessed be Jesus Christ!", she might respond "Amen"; and that she should not approach Jews or Moors or anything related to them, nor should she take anything that they might give her, nor should she speak alone with them. Furthermore, she should kneel before the body of God in church when it is raised, and should know the proper prayers and, at the least, say the Our Father and *Credo in Deum* at that time; and whenever she enters a church or a chapel she should genuflect before the altar and there adore God by saying the Our Father. And so on for similar things.

Moreover, they must teach her not to swear on any account, and if she does so, they should beat her. In addition, she should willingly carry a rosary around her neck and should perform certain vigils in private by herself, and such girls should pray by themselves that God might make them worthy in His service and that He might save them. And, likewise, they should pray for their fathers and their mothers as well as their brothers if they have any, and for their benefactors, living or dead. And as soon as they approach ten or twelve years old, one must make them accustomed to fasting on the principal feast days of the year and on the chief vigils of the Blessed Virgin Mary, and on such occasions, at least, to saying her Life to her, which Life consists of sixty-two Hail Marys, or to saying her Crown, which consists of twelve Hail Marys, and on Friday to saying the Life of Jesus Christ to Him, which amounts to thirty-three Our Fathers. And so on for similar pious prayers.

Second, they must instruct her to honour her father and mother, and to kiss their hands, and to obey their every command and not to argue with them over anything. Moreover, they must teach her to be afraid of them, and often they should awaken in her a great fear of being harmed and at times, if she deserves it, they should administer corporal punishment, though not about the head but behind and on the back with a stick, for Solomon says that the rod is the medicine for the follies of a child. Never should a father or mother show affection to their child if that child is capable of discerning good from evil, but rather they must always teach it about those things of which it should be afraid, although in moderation and without terrifying it.

Third, they must teach her manners, such as the fact that she should always remain silent and speak but little and only when she is asked a question, and that she should avoid saying anything foul or bad mannered, and should not dare to play with youngsters who have nothing to do with her, nor take anything that they might give her, nor play with anyone outside her home or, at least, only with her mother's permission. Likewise, she should learn not to shout when she speaks nor to laugh in a dissolute manner, but discreetly instead. Similarly, her gaze should be trained so that she does not look at anyone directly in the face, but that as soon as she has looked at someone, she should immediately lower her gaze to the floor. And if she has anything to say to a person, she should say it graciously and using few words, all the more so if there are strangers present, and she should not utter false-hoods on any account; and if she commits an indiscretion in public, she should humbly confess her fault to her mother and ask her for-giveness for it. She should never make eyes at any man, nor remain at the window, nor speak from the window to anyone in the street below, particularly young men, for neither a woman who wishes men to lure nor bad apples on the branch shall long endure, as the popular saying goes. And it is the case that, if she becomes accustomed to such habits when she is little, later on it will be impossible to reform her of them. Seneca recommends, in particular, that girls should begin to be raised when they are little, for afterwards, when they have grown, they will not be afraid and, if they have already picked up bad habits, they can never be reformed. [...]

Fifth, parents must teach them not to be slothful, but rather, as much as the circumstances permit, should make them engage in use-ful activities from which, in the future, they might live and by which they might assist their husbands, were fortune to go against them. Policraticus narrates, in the sixth book,[5] that the emperor Octavian made sure his daughters were taught to know everything that it is good for a woman to know, such as working with silk and with wool, and how to make linen and woollen cloth, and how to weave and to sew, and how to spin and how to cut out all types of clothing pertaining to men and to women.

Tullius recounts that a vice-ridden woman of Rome, who never wished to spin but instead advised others not to, went to pay her respects to the empress, namely the wife of the said emperor, Octavian. And the said empress was at that time spinning linen tows and swiftly made many distaffs ready with such tows. And just as the said woman had entered and paid her respects to the empress, she was greatly taken aback at how the empress was spinning and at how she was spinning tows, and when the distaff was given to her so that she and the others with whom she had come might do some spinning, she apologised by saying that she had never done such a thing and nor had any of her companions. And he states in this respect that the empress replied:

"I certainly believe that you are speaking the truth, and it is for this reason that you have such a poor reputation along with all those women who often converse with you, for everyone knows within whose grips lies a woman who does not spin. Therefore, from now on take care not to come into my presence, you or any of your companions, for I am one of those who eagerly spins, and I make my daughters and all my female friends spin as well."

And without further delay, she had her cast out of the palace and made it publicly known that women who did not wish to spin in Rome should be cast out of the city and placed alongside those who do not spin, who reside in brothels. [...]

Sixth, one must teach young girls not to tell untruths. Aristotle says that it is the vice of children to tell lies; however, matters are such that, if it is tolerated in them and becomes a habit of theirs, then later they can never be reformed of it. And this is such a significant vice that, as Scripture says, it brings heavy scorn upon man and renders him hateful to all (Ecclesiasticus 37,23). And if this vice is embodied by a woman, it is in her for ever and renders her most loathsome to her hus-

5 Cf. John of Salisbury, *Policraticus* VI, 4.

band, for it is a great burden to a man that he cannot give credence to
anything that his wife might tell him and it gives him a very good reason to hold her in low esteem. And it is the case that, as soon as a
woman is accustomed to telling lies, then, immediately she has told
them, she fancies that everything is just as she has said, as a result of
which she will not hesitate to corroborate her duplicity with oaths. And
see here how this sin is compounded and increased beyond measure,
and as Scripture says, will bring others in its wake, sins which will ultimately put the woman in great danger. And therefore she must keep
from being false in her words. And it helps a great deal if she is taught
this lesson during her childhood.

Seventh, girls should be taught how to be discreet, and how not to
repeat anything which has been told to them in secret or that they
have seen or heard behind closed doors, and how not to divulge it, for
generally nobody pays attention to children, yet therein lies the danger, however. For as the popular saying goes: "It is children and fools,
they say, who give the game away". They must be told, however, that if
they see or hear any evil acts committed in the home, they should discreetly inform their mother or someone who might find a remedy
without causing scandal to others.

LD 16-17

4.3. *The schooling of maidens*

And you must know in this respect that everything which has been said
above about the raising of girls, must be applied all the more vigor-
ously to maidens insofar as the age of maidens is greater and they
ought to have greater sense, greater modesty and greater fear of God.
Policraticus said that maiden or *domicella* in Latin means the same as
Domini cella, that is to say, the habitation or house of God, for, he says,
since maidens are generally kept under closure, there is no reason to
let their minds be distracted by things from the outside world; thus, if
she has been taught to love God, and purity and chastity in her person, it follows that God abides in her as in a cell and in his house. And
that is what Saint Paul meant when he said, *Prima Corintiorum* VII, *Virgo
cogitat quae Dei sunt ut sit sancta corpore et spiritu* (7,34). And he means
that the good maiden considers and concerns herself with matters
relating to God, and should please God, and be holy and chaste in her
body and worthy in her soul. In other words, she should pray a great

deal and fast frequently and, in particular, she must commend herself to Our Saviour, who was the sovereign and font of virginity; and then to His glorious Mother, who from that glorious font draws out a great ocean of purity, which ocean she pours out over those of her daughters who show devotion to her, and who have her in their memories often or always and who love her dearly.

There are two types of maiden. The first type consists of those who must serve God in a religious order. And so that these learn to read and write more easily, they must enter an order right away, when they are very young. The second type consists of those who intend to marry. And to these Saint Jerome recommends that, much as they may have it in mind to do what their fathers and mothers advise, with respect to their true intentions they should prefer, however, to keep in tact their virginity to God, and come to marriage with some displeasure and reluctance. And such a desire as this will assist them in many things.

LD 19

Saint Ambrose said in his book, *De virginitate*, that a maiden should display humility in her speech, her manner, her attire and her forbearance, for if she is chastised for her vices by those to whom it falls, she should accept it humbly and with great joy, and readily give abundant thanks to the person who has reprimanded her, for that person has shown that he loves her and that he wishes to protect her from evil. The poet Sallustius states that a woman who notices that her daughter is rebellious and that she accepts her chastisement disrespectfully, must either kill her or beat and chasten her so much that she can clearly see that her daughter admits her fault and confesses her guilt and is reformed, in fact, of that very fault. For, if a mother does not act in this way, she will, first of all, make her daughter even more rebellious towards her person than she was before and, consequently, this daughter shall end up having even more scope to commit evil than she had previously, and she will become prouder towards her mother and will scorn her even more when she has left her care. And besides, it puts her at risk of being similarly disrespectful to her husband when she has one, and he, by chance, may punish her in such a manner as is excessive. And Terentius said that a maiden who needs to be chastised beyond her father's walls brings great shame upon her mother, and her mother puts her at great risk, for she will be punished by someone who has no pity for her. Therefore, teach humility to your daughter so that she might be lovable to God and to all those whom she ought please with her agreeable conversation.

LD 23

On how the daughters of sovereigns should be raised

Saturninus, the glorious bishop of Milan, wrote to Gedolph, Duke of Brabant, concerning the upbringing of his children. And he gave him particular instruction regarding how to raise his daughters well, telling him that he should, first of all, keep his daughters from going about a great deal outside their home, for a lot of movement hither and thither presents women with numerous opportunities to commit evil, and removes their sense of shame, for the more a woman is home-loving the greater her modesty, and the more she sees, hears and talks with various people, the less of it she has. And you can see this at a glance in the maidens and ladies at court, for they generally feel no shame at anything because they spend all day among all those people coming and going, and in this way they are more familiar, and on account of this familiarity they let themselves be touched and kissed and felt more readily. And since this is how things are, they get straight down to business if the opportunity presents itself! And therefore he said that chaste women should be completely wild, for just as wild animals do not let people touch them yet domesticated ones let all and sundry pass their hands over them, women, he said, have the choice of being either wild or too familiar.

Second, he advised him never to let his daughters remain idle, but to keep them busy with matters which are permissible, beneficial and pleasing to them so that they do not concern themselves with things which bring shame upon them and carry no advantage, and on account of which they will subsequently suffer great vexation. Works to which women must apply themselves, says this writer, include spinning and weaving. Low-born women, in particular, must devote themselves to their trade, and the low-born and those of middling estate must know how to sew and to cut out what is necessary – for their husbands, themselves and their children – from linen cloth. Noble women must busy themselves with sewing in silk, gold thread and pearls, and with weaving things in gold, braid and silk, and after having woven as much as they need themselves, they must make things for churches also, so that the saints might obtain God's grace for them in forgiveness for the great excesses they commit by showing their flesh to men and turning their bodies into lures by which to seduce men. We have, however, dealt with this particular sin at length in the *Third* book, for which reason we no longer need to speak of it here, for you shall see there how this sin is grievous, and how almighty God punishes it severely in this life and in the next, not only in those women who commit it, but also in those who exercise control over them but who leave them to do as they wish.

Third, he advised him to teach them to observe silence, for their reticence provides evidence of their being chaste and of their not wishing to offer themselves shamelessly to others. And, therefore, men conceive less jealousy towards women who are accustomed to holding their peace than they do towards those who are overconfident or fickle, and they prefer them to be quiet like this and to be somewhat distant and aloof, for they are of greater worth. Second, moreover, their silence does them good service because, in that case, one cannot detect any lack of good sense in them, but instead they seem to be wise, for, as Solomon says, the wise man will hold his peace until the right moment (Ecclesiasticus 20,7). The third reason why their silence is useful is that by remaining silent they do not talk nonsense, which they are in the habit of talking on account of the scant good sense they have. Fourth, by keeping their counsel they never quarrel with anyone; they are thus accustomed to such disputes and well-prepared for them, therefore, if they do not hold their tongues. The fifth reason is that, since they are in the habit of speaking a lot, they utter many falsehoods, which falsehoods render them highly contemptible to men, but, if they say nothing, nobody notices this failing. Sixth, a husband is very glad to have a wife who has been brought up well; for it is very much the case that a woman's good upbringing can be detected most clearly in her reticence. It is obvious then that, for all these reasons, maidens must be well trained in how to remain silent.

Fourth, he informed him that they should be taught to eat properly, for they must eat little in quantity and that little should be eaten elegantly, without raising their eyes and by guiding their hands very skilfully, while always keeping their mouths closed apart from when they are putting in a mouthful. But, above all, they should avoid strong wine and drinking too much, for, as Solomon said, a drunken woman is one of the greatest abominations in this world (Ecclesiasticus 26,11). He told him in addition to bring them up in a manner befitting women, for manly women are worse than any scoundrel in their appearance, speech and bearing, as he himself proves by various examples in his text. And he informed him, in particular, that they should not be prone to falling in love nor should they favour standing by the window, for in that case they are shamelessly offering themselves to men; nor should they become friendly with procurers, for these people make them do ill; and their gaze should be humble and they should never fasten it upon any man; nor should they wish to hear of horrific or villainous acts, for such things cause them to be greatly humiliated if they carry them out, yet render them highly chaste if they abstain from them. And this holy bishop said that maidens should greatly be given to praying and fasting, for that was of considerable use to their bodies and souls. Above all, he advised him to imbue them with a sense of modesty and a love of chastity, so that he might have a hard time persuading them to marry, for maidens who seek a husband on their own account despite the fact that they have someone who is better suited to finding them one and who takes good care of them, are not maidens but brazen hussies with little sense. And if this is the shame of every maiden, it is much more shameful and even worse for the daughters of great lords, who, above all others, should be very sensible, very chaste and very modest.

DC 563

4.4. *Teaching women to read and write*

The afore-mentioned distinguished Doctor and counsellor advises in addition that if you wish to avoid all types of procuring in your home, you must follow these rules. The first is that, if you have a beautiful wife, you should never keep an old and poor female servant within your walls. The reason for this is because it is said that women who are old and poor usually devote themselves to acting as procuresses more than any other people in the world. [...]

The third things is that you should never prohibit your wife from learning to read and write for the following reasons. The first reason is that, if she desires to be wicked, she will not be able to restrain herself if she cannot read and write. The next reason is that a woman who is able to do this is of much greater worth than if she is not, and can serve God by reciting the hours of the Passion and of the Virgin Mary and other fine prayers; she can occupy herself more easily in church by reading and praying, just as women in France and other parts of the world do, and she can better and more knowingly serve her husband and assist his family, as well as remain more easily at home reading various books which deal with the salvation of her soul.

TC 625

On how one must teach maidens and women to read and write

However, the said emperor proved to him by means of the following reasons that the one to whom it falls should teach all manner of things to every person beloved to him. And the first reason was that, if one were to refrain from this on the grounds that such learning might present that person with the opportunity for doing wrong, it follows that, for this same reason, one would also have to take away from a woman all those things which might be the cause or opportunity of her acting sinfully. And, as a result, everyone would have to shut his woman indoors at all times and keep her in such a manner that she never left the house nor spoke to anyone nor went to see anyone, for all of these things can be an opportunity for her to commit sins, all of which comments are highly foolish and out of place.

The second reason is that whoever considers the good which can pass to a woman from such knowledge, must not pay heed all the time to the evil, for if a woman knows how to read, she will be prepared to offer up many prayers, which is a reason why we can presume that God will protect her from evil; and, besides, by reading, she will avoid much idleness, which will protect her from sin. Likewise, by reading she can inform herself about the virtuous life from various good books which she may read and which will protect her from evil. Similarly, by reading she will better be fitted to speaking, thinking and reasoning, and advising her husband or her children or any other person dear to her.

The third reason is that the more calm and home-loving a woman is the more she is commended, and nothing can calm her more at home than that she find some edifying thing in which she can take great delight, and these things can be noteworthy books and such as women might be inclined to read.

The fourth reason is that women are usually angry, melancholic and lacking in great resolve, and there is nothing in this world as effective in enabling them to correct the said passions as good books and the sayings of the saints and Holy Scripture.

The fifth reason is that usually women are very emotional and sad and suffer great heartache, and having good books is a sovereign remedy for putting these things out of their minds.

The sixth reason is that it befits a woman to live sagely and to behave herself and run her household sensibly, and to give instruction to her sons and daughters and her domestic servants. And how better can she do all of this than if she has learnt from fine books? Without doubt, by no other means can it be done so well!

The seventh reason is that one should devote greater efforts to ensuring that everybody does good than to preventing a certain few from doing wrong, and one should not take the good things away from the good people on account of those who act badly. Otherwise, never would a sovereign have instituted laws, for laws have been the occasion for many to break the law; however the law is no less valid on this account. And, in brief, all that which is commonly said and done can be the occasion for evil; however, one does not desist from doing that which is commonly done and must be done on account of this alone.

The eighth reason is that, if you only concentrate on the negative aspects, a person could sooner beguile an ignorant woman than a well-read woman with the same level of intelligence, and this would likewise occur with two men of similar intelligence, for sooner could one decive an ignorant than a knowledgeable man.

The ninth reason is that women have very many shortcomings and are very difficult to reform, for, since they are haughty and proud, they reject, by nature, every attempt that is made to mend their ways. It is, therefore, a good remedy to reform them through the study of worthy books, for this form of correction does not make them lose their temper or become angry with anyone, but instead they accept it without any loss of composure.

The tenth reason is that, as Saint Jerome has said, there is as great a difference between a knowledgeable and an ignorant person as there is between light and darkness and, as a result, whoever loves a person dearly must lead her to the light of true wisdom and free her from the darkness of ignorance.

And, for these reasons, the said emperor wanted men to teach their wives, daughters and close female relatives to read and write as well as to instruct them in various useful kinds of learning.

DC 554

On how the manners of women from other nations are not in all cases exemplary and on how it is good for women to be able to read

While King Robert, in our days the king of Sicily and of Naples, was alive, certain French nobles came to Naples with their wives and entire families. And as certain high-born Neapolitans learnt to dress in the manner of those Frenchmen, namely to wear scanty, tight-fitting, and less than chaste clothing, so the ladies of the court and of the said city wished to resemble those French ladies who had come there by wearing skimpy and tight-fitting apparel like them, and to dance all the time, and to drink in the streets, and to go riding just like a man, and endlessly to kiss and embrace men in public, and to sing twittering songs in French as the noble ladies do in France, and to speak of love affairs and falling in love and to swap jokes with young people as was their way.

And in those times there was a saintly queen in that place, called Sancia, the wife of the said King Robert, who was the daughter of the king of Majorca. And she was a woman of great holiness and great reputation, who, after the death of her husband, subsequently went to her grave a Poor Clare, in the monastery of Saint Clare, in Naples. [...] This saintly queen said that the other women who were not French should learn the following things from France, namely to keep their bosom covered and to go to church with a book in their hand and to read from this without pause and without looking up, and to honour their husband, and to raise their children well. The other things which were not virtuous were best left to the devil. In this respect, you must know that the said holy queen strongly advised and set store by the fact that every woman should know how to read, for she said that they would have more opportunity to be devout, to occupy themselves, to find out about every kind of good, to remain at home more and to console themselves during their tribulations. And she said that men who, in order to protect their wives more effectively, did not wish them to be able to read, were very foolish, since to be able to read and to read a great deal gave women an opportunity to acquaint themselves with much that was good and to do good more than anything else, for being able to read gives women the said advantages. And she said that, beyond this, husbands could maintain private correspondence with them more easily than if they were not able to read, for, if they are not able to and their husband writes to them, someone else necessarily has to know what he has written. And, if they wish to be wicked, good books can more effectively dissuade them from being so than reading letters which arrive for them can impel them to act wickedly, for even in the absence of letters, such wickedness can be perpetrated by means of signals and words both coded and overt between each person, for which letters are not necessary.

LD 56

5. The schooling of children

5.1. *The vices and virtues of children*

On how one can know other people according to twelve natural passions

Seventh, a sovereign must consider the age of his subjects in his judgements and in his governance, for young people are more inclined towards some passions, impulses or proclivities and old people towards others, for, according to what this writer states – and this is likewise affirmed by Aristotle *in secundo Rhetoricorum* – young people have six commendable habits. For, first of all, they are generous, and this is the case because they obtain things without effort or intelligence.

Second, they have great hopes of attaining that which they desire, and this is the case because they are ardent and fiery, and they cannot imagine that anything might obstruct them; it is also the case because they have never encountered great impediments and they do not know how much trouble it takes to acquire something one does not already possess. They take pleasure, moreover, only in what they can see and what they anticipate and in nothing from the past, for they have seen and done little in past times, and, therefore, they place great hope in the future.

Third, they have lively minds and strong wills, and they are made so by the great fieriness within them, which inclines them to soar above all other people and to obtain glory and honour.

Fourth, they are unable to see as many dangers in things as lie concealed, for they imagine – since they know little and have seen little – that everyone is honourable and just.

Fifth, they are merciful, for they are unable to assess the evil that anyone has committed, and they abhor all punishment and love pleasure, and, therefore, when they see that others are in danger of suffering or are, in fact, in the process of suffering punishment, they are immediately moved to mercy. For this reason, Philadelphus, the Turkish emperor, ordained that no young person should ever be called to serve in a criminal court for they are always thinking of ways to relieve the suffering of the accused and they never pay heed to the offence committed.

Sixth, they are easily aroused to shame, for, since on account of their ardour they desire to be honoured and held in esteem, if they fall into disrepute, therefore, they experience great displeasure, and that displeasure is linked with shame. And for this reason, the writer Hermes says that every sovereign should do his very best to acquire such commendable characteristics himself when he is young and, therefore, should know how to govern young people in the light of the said six virtuous tendencies they possess.

According to the same authors, however, young people have six or seven other shortcomings which are worthy of censure. And the first is that they slavishly follow their passions and inclinations. And they do this because they are very fiery and greatly lacking in reason, and, therefore, their fieriness impels them to follow their passions and their scant reason does not hold them back. And therefore they are very lecherous and quickly moved to anger.

The second is that they are very mutable. And, according to the Philosopher *in secundo Rhetoricorum,*[6] the reason is because, being fiery, their humours are in furious motion, and, since the soul follows the body's passions, it follows that their wills and their appetites are likewise set in motion at once. Therefore, Aristotle says in this respect that young people covet things keenly but are soon sated, whereby they seek something else.

The third is that they place their faith in people too readily and this is because, since they are not particularly conversant with the various guiles of man, they imagine that everyone is telling them the truth.

The fourth is that they are soon moved to defame others. And the reason is that, as has been mentioned, they wish to outdo others on account of their natural fieriness, and since no one accords much honour to the young as a result of their shortcomings and their youth, they therefore consider themselves to be scorned forthwith and so immedi-

[6] Cf. Aristotle, *Rhetoric* II, 12.

ately inveigh against others. The philosopher Lelius recounts that, since young men desire above all else to appear highly illustrious to women, and all the more so to those that they love, the greatest insult and offence, therefore, that a young man can receive is that he be disgraced and upbraided in front of a woman or women of whom he is fond.

The fifth is that they greatly covet being held in esteem, and on account of their fieriness and ardour they utter things which are excessive and harsh, and since they do not know themselves, for they have no great learning, they presume, therefore, that they know many things of which they are ignorant. And for this reason, they say everything that comes into their heads and, thinking that they speak the truth, they give it their warrant with such obstinacy that, against their will, they are bound to utter many falsehoods. And, once they have uttered them, they are fearful that they will be taken to be liars, and, therefore, they uphold them as obstinately as they can. The said philosopher says that a young man of his day was greatly taken to task because he affirmed and endorsed in this manner the falsehood that he had uttered, and because he uttered it without a trace of doubt so as not to be taken for a liar. And he says that the young man replied that, by his faith, once he had uttered the falsehood, his mind latched onto it to such a degree and with such ardour, that it seemed to him that he could swear with certainty that it was as he had said. See then, says the aforesaid philosopher, how much danger there is in a young person's becoming accustomed to uttering falsehoods, for so deep is the imprint they leave that these young people can never forsake them, but rather will defend them unto death.

The sixth is that they are prone to telling untruths, as is proved by the fifth point we have just described. And the said philosopher attributes another reason to this fact, and it is this, namely that young people are very lively on account of their ardour, and they are inclined to say and do many things, and, since they know little, it follows that by speaking and acting with great ardour they are bound to utter many falsehoods in order to cast their words and deeds in a favourable light. The great philosopher, Cicero, therefore, informed his children that they should never believe anything told them by young men, for, at the drop of a hat, they would promise heaven and earth in order to attain what they desired and would utter a thousand falsehoods in order to lend colour to their words. And, in this respect, he tells of Olibama, the wife of King Siroch of Safira in the east, who would let out puffing sounds whenever her husband spoke to her, for she had noticed that when he spoke he always sang his own praises to her and attributed many things to himself that he had never said or done. And when her husband noticed her puffing and asked her why she puffed so heavily when he was speaking to her, she replied to him that the westerly wind did not pick up from the opposite direction as soon as the easterly wind had dropped, for, if it did, the sky would have rotated too quickly and thus the entire world would be lost in a puff of air. And by way of explaining what she had told him, she said the following:

"My lord, your empty speeches are like wind in my face, by which, if I were to believe them, you would make me lose my mind, and in this manner, between us, we would commit so many follies that our governance of this kingdom would be less effective and would then lead to our complete downfall." [7]

And the king, who realised that she was aware that he had been telling her nothing but lies, said to her:

"May the blessings of God be upon you, my wife, who have so wittily reformed me of my vice!"

And from then on he was careful not to do the same again.

The seventh shortcoming is that they are not careful about anything they do, but everything they do, they carry out with great ardour, so that what they love, they love with great ardour, and what they detest, they detest with a vengeance. Similarly, if they praise or censure anything, or honour or dishonour it, they do it all to great excess. And this is on account of their great natural fieriness and ardour and the little control they have over their scant good sense and their paltry powers of reason.

DC 814

---

7 A sustained and untranslatable play on words: besides the primary meaning of Cat. *bufar*, namely 'to blow' (of the wind, etc.), it also means to puff; Cat. *buf*, therefore, means the blowing of the wind or the act of puffing, and the air that is thereby expelled from the mouth, but it also means 'a very brief period of time or instant', whereby the final clause of the queen's witticism (Cat. *així es perdria tot lo món en un buf*) also means 'the entire world would be lost in an instant'.*

5.2. *General rules for the schooling of children and adolescents*

5.2.1. *How to live*

A chapter which shows how fathers and mothers should instruct their children in the knowledge of God

Instruction, which, as has been stated, is the third good thing owed to children according to Fulgentius, resides in this, he says, namely that fathers and mothers should educate their sons and daughters in the knowledge of God and should teach them the Our Father, the Hail Mary and the *Credo in Deum*. They should also put them in the habit of going to church and to confession and of not swearing in God's name, and of willingly attending mass and doing so devoutly and of not keeping company with wicked people. And, in addition to this, they must teach them to earn themselves a living in accordance with their station, namely to be skilled in some worthy profession or field of knowledge which they might practise as an antidote to every kind of idleness or in order better to earn their living. And they must insist that this knowledge or profession be righteous and not akin to sin, so that they might not always live under the wrath of God nor come to a bad end. And with this aim in mind, then, says Fulgentius, the first three years during which Holy Scripture is reticent about the deeds of Jesus Christ can be of use to us, for they teach us, as has been said, to know what we ought to do with children who are of the said age that Our Saviour was at that time, namely, between eight and twelve years old.

VC 5, 2

On what one must give the young children of sovereigns to eat and drink, and in what things they must be trained and educated

Greek philosophy alludes to the fact, and it is stated by Aristotle in the seventh book of his *Politics*,[8] that one must not give wine to small children to drink at the outset, while they are still suckling, for they say that this greatly predisposes them to contracting illnesses, especially leprosy; but one should feed them on soft and moist foods until the age of seven, for such things are transmuted swiftly and easily in them. And if their mothers cannot suckle them, one must seek out a wet-

---

[8] Cf. *Politics* VII, 17.

nurse for them whose complexion[9] is similar to that of their mother. And he says that it is beneficial for them if, at that time, one accustoms them to undergoing periods of moderate coldness, for they are more healthy as a result of this and their muscles are better prepared for military pursuits. And, therefore, he says that in certain regions they bathe small children in rivers, for the cold makes their muscles firmer and keeps their natural heat within.

He says, likewise, that moderate movement is beneficial for them, since as a result of this they are more healthy and they are not slothful in the future and it aids them in their digestion and, consequently, it allows them to grow more rapidly and makes their limbs stronger. And, therefore, he says that one should make them certain instruments with which they can play and, while they play they should move about and exert themselves with delight, and then one should entertain them by distracting them and inspiring them to play and move themselves. Also, one should sing in front of them and induce them to sing along softly; but one must not let them cry, for in crying they expend much energy and lose their strength, and often they exhaust themselves by their crying and grow very sad, with the result that they could suffer death from frequent crying.

He also says that the more a child grows, the more must he devote himself to suitable activities, such as the art of combat or the throwing of spears and stones. And Aristotle says that one must always take care that a child has a fit and healthy body, and this can be achieved through moderate physical activity and by living in the way that has been stated. In addition, he says that one must ensure that they respect their parents and honour their elders, and see to it that they have worthy intentions and that they are well mannered. And he says that one must already teach them this during the first seven years of their lives.

And, according to the Holy Fathers of old, during the second seven-year period they must be taught some or all of the said sciences, according to their aptitude, inclination and temperament, and they should be made acquainted with God and taught to make the sign of the cross, to say the Our Father, the I Believe and the Hail Mary, and to stretch out their hands when the precious body of Jesus Christ is raised, and so on for the other things that are common among Christians, and they must be taught to flee all heathens like the plague.

9 In the medieval sense of physical constitution (consisting of the four humours).*

And Aristotle gives this law for raising children, namely that one must continually ensure, either by habit or by custom, that they are so used to doing good that they do it more out of habit than on rational grounds, for at that time their powers of reason are slight, and habit makes up for reason; and, subsequently, when they have acquired reason, they become aware that their inclination or habit is good and then they do it willingly. He says in this particular respect that, once they have passed their fourteenth year, children have some degree of reason, and at this time it is necessary, on account of the carnal desires which are already awakening in them, for one to preserve them most intently from eating and drinking too much. And, further, they must not go to indecent or suspect places in order to commit foul carnal acts, and, further still, they should be humble and obedient to their parents; and this is important, says Aristotle in this regard, on account of the great compliance that children owe them. [...]

He advises people of all stations in this particular respect, moreover, always to make young men and boys undergo strenuous exercise, for he says that through moderate exertion the body becomes warm, which warmth consumes the noxious superfluities that lie within them. And besides this, through such exertions they avoid idleness and every vice which springs from it, and they are distracted from engaging in and devoting themselves to other wicked occupations, and it makes the body better prepared for military pursuits.

He says, however, *in octavo Politicorum*[10] that since physical and intellectual effort are mutually opposed, and since the muscles of workers become very strong on account of their work, therefore strong muscles greatly impede the efforts of the mind for, as he says himself *in secundo De anima*,[11] those whose muscles are weak are more suited to having lofty thoughts than others. On account of this, he advocates that, once they have sufficient training in military matters, the first-born sons of sovereigns who are destined to govern should not devote themselves continually to strenuous exercise, so that they may attend to the moral sciences more readily, which sciences teach one to govern wisely, for, as Solomon says, it is better to be wise than to have weapons of war (Eccl 9,18). And if the son of a great lord is skilled at arms, as well as shrewd and bold, he is worth a hardy knight, but if he

[10] Cf. *Politics* VIII, 4.
[11] Cf. *De anima* II, 9, 421a 25-26.

is wise he is worth ten thousand of them, for wisdom is of infinitely greater benefit in feats of arms than strength. And, therefore, he says that it is better for such young men to attend mainly to governance rather than their physical strength. And this is in harmony with what he states in the prologue to the *Politics*,[12] namely that nature gives strong and robust limbs to combatants and servants so that they can toil effectively, but it is not primarily a question of giving such strength to sovereigns, but rather of giving them understanding and wisdom by means of which they might be able to govern others.

DC 562

On how to raise children in their infancy

The education of children consists, in short, of the following points, according to what is stated by Macarius Vercellensis in his *De doctrina parvulorum*; and he says in this respect that a child should, first of all, be taught to be fearful, especially of his father and his teacher, for mothers are rarely feared, to their great discredit. And also they should be brought up to know the Our Father, the Hail Mary and the *Credo in Deum*, and to say grace and to give thanks to God at the end of a meal. And, in addition, they should be instructed to pay special respect to their father and mother and to their grandfather and grandmother, by kissing their hands and bowing low to them and removing their hats. Furthermore, they should know how to maintain a modest appearance and to behave themselves. Similarly, they should be taught to remain silent at all times in front of other adults. Also, they should know how to speak respectfully and sensibly. And, in addition, they should know how to feed themselves and to abstain from food and to drink little and only wine which is heavily diluted, and to avoid eating sweets, and uttering foul words and swearing, and to keep their distance from all bad company; and they should be taught the habit of greatly welcoming words of instruction and preaching and lessons, and of respecting, honouring and giving thanks to those who chastise them.

And he advises on this very matter that girls should be well brought up, and especially given to praying, to fasting and abstinence, to politeness, and to a fondness for enclosure. And on no account

[12] Cf. *Politics* I, 2.

should they be idle or talkative or prone to falling in love; rather they should relish chastity and avoid using make-up, and readily conceal their faces and wear modest clothing, and they should be humble and reserved, and should be able to treat everyone with reverence and honour who merits such. And they should be aware of what they must love, and how they must serve their loved ones according to their rank and kinship, and they should allow themselves to be married only with some reluctance.

Saint Jerome says, *Epistola* XCV, that there is no way at all of estimating how much merit lies in a father's and a mother's raising their children well, for he says that in young people what the poet Aspasius states is true, namely *Quod nova testa capit, inveterata sapit,* or, in other words, whatever a young mind takes in it will always retain, even when it is old. Saint Gregory, *in septimo* of his *Register,*[13] advises that children should be taught to be obedient, that they should not tell falsehoods on any account and should always be occupied with something, and that they should not keep company with nor learn from dissolute tutors or teachers, for the vices of these men are often transmitted to the children. And in this respect the child's father and mother, he says, can ensure that, as their child grows up, he thus profits increasingly from learning what is permissible and from avoiding wickedness, especially the common types of wickedness, such as lust, greed and sloth, and those who are fond of these things. And besides, says this writer, if a father and mother are given to any vice at all, they must conceal this from their children as best they can, in order that the latter should not on any account follow their bad example and that they might hold them in greater respect; and, furthermore, so that their sins do not harm their children in this life, as they sometimes do, according to what is stated in the sixty-first Distinction, *Si gens anglorum,*[14] although Scripture says that the son shall not be damned on account of the sin that the father has committed, rather the sin will be upon the father (Ezek 18,20).

DC 791

---

[13] Cf. Gregorius Magnus, *Registrum epistolarum* VII, 23.
[14] *Decretales* I, 56, 10.

5.2.2. *Study programme*

What sovereigns should ensure that their children are taught

People, especially sovereigns, must teach their children first of all the *Credo in Deum* and everything that is related to the faith in general, and to offer prayers to God and to say the Our Father and the Hail Mary, and to say a few prayers in church, and devoutly to adore the precious body of Jesus Christ, and to go to confession at times, and to refrain from swearing and lying, and to honour their father and mother, for when they learn such things during their infancy, they do them later on without realising.

They should, moreover, make sure that they are taught good manners and good habits, for at such an age dissolute impulses and capricious desires arise in children, for which reason they must be resisted at that time above all. And all the more so because Aristotle says: *Principiis obsta,*[15] which means that one must meet evil head on at the earliest opportunity in order to eradicate it, and one should not rely upon doing this when one is old for then is not the best time to abandon it. And Aristotle gives an example of this in *secundo Rhetoricorum,* namely the example of the freshly cut stick, which straight away bends in the place that one wishes it to but, when it is dry, can no longer be curved.[16] And especially, he says, because at that stage, namely during their infancy, children are better disposed to retaining and imprinting upon themselves every kind of thing that they are taught or told. And Solomon, *Proverbiorum* XXII, is in agreement with this when he says *Adolescens iuxta viam suam; etiam cum senuerit, non recedet ab ea* (22,6). And he means this, namely that a young man will follow that path he has been shown in his youth for, once he has grown accustomed to it, he will never completely depart from it.

And the writer Seneca states that children, and especially the children of sovereigns, must learn Latin grammar, so that they are able, at the very least, to speak competently to any foreigner who might be presented to them and is acquainted with it, and so that they may not be misled by letters that they send or receive on account of the ruses or malice of scribes. And so that he knows it more fully, he must already start to learn it during his childhood and youth. Furthermore, if a sov-

[15] The phrase is, in fact, from Ovid; cf. *Remedia amoris,* ll. 91-92.
[16] The work here mentioned does not contain this image, although it can be found, for example, in the commentary by Martí de Viciana to Aristotle's *Economics* II, 3.

ereign's son knows Latin, he can study many books which are difficult
to understand and are suitable for his learning how to govern, which
books he would not understand if he was not conversant with Latin.
And likewise, since human nature is inclined to every kind of evil, it is
therefore necessary for the sons of sovereigns to devote themselves to
Latin and to other sciences from the quadrivium right from the outset, so that they do not give any thought to learning about villainy and
tyranny and many other evil things. Likewise, as has been said earlier,
sovereigns above all other men must be learned and virtuous so as better to govern others. Therefore, it is necessary for them to be
acquainted with the kind of learning and lore from which they might
find out about useful forms of knowledge and wise governance and
also learn how to live virtuously. From all this, they might come to
appreciate what true governance is and how tyranny is an evil thing, of
danger to every sovereign, with a view to their being able to avoid it
and to preserve themselves, their households, their children and their
kind. And, besides, when the people see how the sons of their sovereigns are devoting themselves to wisdom and to worthwhile forms of
knowledge, they shall begin to revere them for it all the more during
their youth, and shall hold them in higher esteem and anticipate their
lordship and governance with greater desire, joy and expectation.

Furthermore, they must teach them to write, for writing is
immeasurably useful to great lords insofar as they often need to write
certain things down in order to remember them and so that nobody
else knows about them; thus they write about family matters to other
men, which matters, if they were known by anybody else, would cause
great danger. For this reason, Alfarabius said *in suo Rudimentario* that
sons have a right to lodge a civil complaint about the poor level of
education they have received from their father if he has not, at the
very least, taught them to read and write and to understand Latin as
well, for without these things a man is as a fool among the people of
the world. And he tells the tale of the Roman emperor Arcadius, who
had his daughters fully educated in the said matters, for he said that
worthy forms of knowledge should be transmitted to all those whom
one loves. And since, on one occasion, he states, a great knight said
to him that it was not good for a woman to know such things, the
emperor proved to him by means of various arguments that preventing a woman from knowing such things had its roots in great wickedness and in men's poor judgement and great suspicion, for these

men imagine that such learning might be the occasion of great evil to them.

DC 553

What the sons of sovereigns must learn when they are children

The great philosophers thought it highly desirable that kings' sons should learn logic, in order that they might be able to discern readily those who come to speak to them using trustworthy arguments. They also recommended the study of rhetoric, so that these princes might be able to propose, assess or dismiss any matter by means of arguments which are clear, simple and intelligible to the people. Furthermore, they approved of their learning the principles of arithmetic and geometry alone, in order that they might spend their time profitably and put their intellects to the test in many affairs which are often necessary to sovereigns, who, since they have to attend to practically everything, must be informed and assisted from all sides. Similarly, they can learn about optics, which teaches them about what is seen by one's bodily eyes, and also about music and instruments which, after one's exertions, offer the heart permissible pleasures; and this science is heartily recommended by the Philosopher in the eighth book of his *Politics*.[17] And, besides this, it is very good for them to be acquainted with astrology so that they can take care of their health and do their job better for, although all good derives from God, He has, nevertheless, entrusted many things with the governance of the causes here below, such as the heavens and the stars and the planets. For this reason, in the past, after making their invocations to God, the kings of old would have people study at important and dangerous junctures the astrological conjunctions affecting their affairs, and this practice worked very well for them. And it would also be highly useful to do this now more than ever; however, there would be a great danger that, on account of man's great wickedness, people might forsake all confidence in God and follow the stars and worship them in order to resolve their problems.

The said philosophers also advocated that sovereign's sons should be made familiar with the principles of natural philosophy, metaphysics, medicine and theology, for they could learn all this in a short space of time. And in addition to all this, they should devote them-

---

[17] See Aristotle, *Politics*, especially VIII, 3 and 5.

selves, above all, to moral philosophy in order to acquire virtues, and similarly they should study the laws and charters of their kingdom or lordship as well as the ecclesiastical canons, in order more readily to pursue justice in the absence of weighty advice from others. They were also in favour of their being skilfully taught all there is to be known about feats of arms, and that they might learn swordsmanship at home, and that with the assistance of good teachers, good books and much experience they should continually devote themselves to military pursuits. However, they did not endorse their being taught the art of composing songs or writing verse, for learning this would severely distract them from other more necessary things, and time is short and this kind of knowledge is not of great benefit and entices those who read poetry into falling in love and that serves no purpose at all. And he says that those who teach the sons of sovereigns must pay heed to the sciences or arts towards which the said children are more inclined and must give them greater instruction in those, but above all in wisdom, the art of combat and the histories and annals of their predecessors, which they must know by heart.

DC 555

The *Historia latina* recounts that when Julius Caesar heard that Aurelius, his nephew, whom he had made king of Thessaly, spent almost all his time studying and performing astrology and alchemy and amusing himself, he wrote the following to him:

> My nephew, I deeply regret having made you king, since you do not know how to govern yourself nor, as a result, are you capable of governing others. Do you not know that a king is placed in a position of governance so that, exclusively or primarily, he might administer justice and maintain peace among his people? Yet you have undertaken things which are the province of indolent youths and mad people and inveterate rogues! I tell you and swear to you, by God in heaven, that if, once you have read this present letter, you do not cast all those mad books of yours which you are currently studying into a fire and do not devote yourself to the justice of your people, to which end I made you king, then I shall immediately take back your kingdom and put you to death. For I am very ashamed that a person from my family should be as unsuited to and incapable of governing as you, and

that, having abandoned your principal office, which is to administer justice, for which there is never sufficient time, you have given yourself over to follies and to things which can be of no benefit whatsoever in the administration of justice.

And the account states in this respect that the said king, reading the emperor's command and realising the soundness of his arguments, immediately abandoned all the said things which were an impediment to him and henceforth administered justice remarkably well.

DC 582

5.2.3. *Training the body*

What bearing a sovereign must have

Andronicus also made a third recommendation to the said sovereign, and it was this, namely that every sovereign should keep a close eye upon his bearing. And, in this particular respect, he states that the reason why he said this was because a man can reveal a lack of good sense or great pride and great impropriety in his bearing yet, by chance, he may be completely free of such things. However, it would set less of a bad example to have such vices and not to display them through one's mannerisms than to display them even though one did not, in fact, suffer from them at all. And he said the following, namely that sovereigns must endeavour to assign a task to each limb and to prevent any of these limbs from involving themselves in the task of another. By way of example, it is certainly the proper task of man's feet, legs and thighs to move and to transport him when he walks; so, what need is there, he says, when a person is in motion, for him to move one side this way and the other side that way and to wave his arms about just like a madman? Similarly, when a person needs to turn around and his body is at rest, it is the proper task of the head and neck to turn itself in the direction of where it is required to turn; so, what madness is it, if a person wishes to turn around, for him to turn his whole body and his neck and head as well, just as if it were rigid and all of a piece, or as if it were nothing other than a full packsaddle or a piece of timber? Similarly, it is the proper task of ears to hear; so, what madness is it for someone to open their mouth when they wish to hear something? Similarly, it is the proper task of the mouth and the tongue to speak; so, what need is there for a man who is speaking to move his head, arms, hands, feet and eyes and to beat himself upon every part of his body? Similarly, the proper task of the knee is to kneel; so, what need is there for a man who is kneeling to lie down on his side and to roll around and display the mannerisms typical of a madman?

It is clear, then, this writer says, that sovereigns and their sons should be properly schooled when it comes to their bearing so that they are taken to be wise and are held in great respect. And he said that a great lord's dignity and good sense lay in his bearing, and that there should not be great movements of his body while he was walking or standing still but that his gait should be sure and his gaze circumspect. Further, he should not raise his head to look at windows nor speak a great deal in the company of others, but rather he should leave this to others or briefly deal with matters that were put to him. Similarly, he should not laugh much, for it was sufficient to show happiness upon his face, and he should never display either very great joy or very great consternation in the company of others, unless extreme or acute circumstances arose. And he says that, in particular, sovereigns must avoid feminine gestures and language and anything that might render him contemptible to his people.

DC 559

6. THE EDUCATION OF SERVANTS

The *Historia latina* narrates that during the time of the Roman emperor Phocas, one could hardly find any servants or maids. And the reason was that as soon as the young sons of common serving men had reached maturity they wished to do as they pleased, and they did not wish to serve anyone, but all of them together became great rogues who played games of chance and gambled. Likewise, the young girls who were daughters of common men did not wish to work as maids. And the reason was that when they were of a marriageable age, they asked for alms throughout the town in order to be able to pay their dowries, or their fathers or mothers handed them over to some nobleman who would keep them for a year or six months as his concubine and would then marry them. And, in this way, none of them wished to work as maids. [...]

Eulogius, who was a great *iurisconsultus*, also states that Pirrus, the king of Rome, issued a decree in favour of servants, saying that every man in the position of artisan who had a stripling or a young man under the age of thirty as his servant, was obliged to teach him a trade by which he could live. And, if he were a man from the city without a trade himself, he was obliged to teach him to read and write perfectly, to serve a lord, to wait at table, to serve in a household and to tend horses, and he was bound to teach him how to knead dough, to cook, to play musical instruments, to practice swordsmanship, to jump, to dance, to sing, to speak courteously and to conduct himself according to his station. And those who had serving maids were obliged to guarantee their physical integrity, so that, if they were raped, these people would be deserving of capital punishment and, depending on the decision of the authorities, they would be bound to compensate them at a rate fixed by these same.

DC 340

EDUCATION AT SCHOOL

IV

1. ON THE SENSE OF HEARING

1.1. *A chapter which teaches to whom we must listen*

We must now look at the fourth principal point of this *Treatise on the sense of hearing*, and it is that we should consider to whom we must listen. And you should be aware that the saints state that we must listen, in particular, to six types of speaker, namely, to preachers; and, second, to one's parents; third, to one's teachers; fourth, to one's friends; fifth, to the elderly; and sixth, to anyone who speaks well.

The first, then, are the preachers. And one should be aware that when we consider that a preacher is God's messenger, and is sent to us to inform us about the path of truth, and we realise that the word of God which he is bound to proclaim tells us what we must do, and he rouses us to abandon sin and to uphold God's commandments, and he teaches us to make our way to paradise, we should rush to hear him with all the willingness we can muster, having set everything else to one side. See with what willingness we rush to hear news about the people we love and how we receive their letters and their greetings with great delight. Oh, and how much more willingly should we hasten to listen to the person who speaks to us of our leader and of Him who is our friend above all other friends, namely Our Lord God and His glorious son, Jesus Christ! But it is a fact that the love which we show Him is so paltry and the concern which we show for the salvation of our souls so slight, that we have no appetite for things connected with God, which is a very bad sign, as Jesus Christ said, *Iohannis* VIII, using these words: *Qui ex Deo est verba Dei audit, propterea vos non auditis, quia ex Deo non estis. Vos ex parte diabolo estis* (8,47). And it means precisely this, addressing those who listen to Him unwillingly and with scant inclination: He who is of God willingly listens to the word of God and, therefore, you do not listen to it willingly, because you are not of God, but rather of the devil, who is your father and rules over and governs you. Therefore you cannot listen to anything connected with God. Saint Augustine says that among the signs which most suggest that somebody is predestined for salvation is that he willingly listens to the word of God, and, on the contrary, among the greatest signs from which we can surmise that somebody is predestined for damnation, is that he does not wish to listen to the word of God. [...]

1.2. *Another chapter concerning those to whom we must listen*

Secondly, we must also listen to our fathers and mothers on account of the respect that we owe them according to human nature and according to God's commandment, Who instructs us to honour them. And besides this, we must listen to them because we can assume that the love which they bear us is so great, that they would never give us anything other than good guidance. And for this reason, Solomon said, *Proverbiorum* I: Hear, my son, your father's instruction and forget not your mother's teaching so that, on account of the respect you have shown them and the blessings they have given you, God might bestow His grace upon you, which shall last you forever and help you profit from all that is good (1,8-9). It is true, however, that, at times, parents greatly inspire their children to a love of the world and its vanities, and in that case one should neither listen to them nor believe them for, although in other senses one is obliged to honour them, in this respect not, however; Our Saviour says, instead, that he who loves Him should disregard and abhor any advice which comes from one's father and mother or any other person and which contradicts the Lord's commandments (Mt 10, 37). And He says this because they have an infinitely greater obligation to the supreme father, who is Our Lord God, than to any other.

1.3. *A third chapter concerning those to whom we must listen*

We must also listen to our teachers with every eagerness, in accordance with what the third point alluded to, and we must do so because they enlighten us with their teachings and are the source of all that is useful to us. And, therefore, Aristotle says in his *Ethics* that *Magistris, diis et parentibus non potest equivalens reddi.*[1] And he means that nobody can render sufficient recompense to God or to his parents or teachers. Therefore, the poet said that one of the portals to wisdom was respect for one's teachers. We read that Hippocrates gave the order that in his school nobody should dare refute or dismiss anything until he had attended classes for seven years, for Aristotle says: *Oportet ad discentem credere.*[2] And he means that he who is learning must believe what his teacher tells him and must not undertake to refute anything, but must persuade his mind to believe what his teacher tells him. However, if the pupil has cause to refute the master's teaching on some matter, it is permissible for him to ask him respectfully and to seek an answer.

The fourth point teaches us that we must listen to our friends for the reason that they are one's second self, according to what Seneca states, and are such that they are worthy of always being listened to insofar as they have given you their love and their hearts, which are the most precious things a man has. [...] However, he notes in this respect that a true friend will almost never address pleasant words to you; instead, it is a fact that you will never hear agreeable words from him. The reason for this is that so much is the fervour and true love of a genuine friend aroused towards the one he loves, that he is always afraid that the person he loves might make a mistake in a certain respect. And, therefore, a true friend, in general, always reproaches and chastises the one he loves, and since hardly anyone ever likes to receive a rebuke, this is the reason why one will never hear pleasing words from a friend. However, whoever possesses good sense must always listen to the chastisements and harsh words of a friend as if they were the words of an angel in heaven, for they are all spoken out of love and with a view to the great benefit of him to whom they are spoken. And Solomon, therefore, said, *Proverbiorum: Meliora sunt vulnera diligentis quam fraudulenta oscula odientis* (27,6). And he means that better are the blows of a friend than the sweet and deceitful words of an enemy.

[1] *Ethica ad Nicomachum* IX, 1.
[2] Cf. *De sophisticis elenchis* 2, 165b 3

1.4. A fourth chapter concerning those to whom we must listen

The fifth point is that you must listen to those who are elderly, for Scripture states, as is believed by practically everybody, that wisdom is with the aged (Job 12,12). And, therefore, *Ecclesiasticus, capitulo* XI, states that *In medio seniorum ne adicias loqui* (11,8).[3] And it means to advise you who are younger never to dare speak in the midst of such elderly people, but rather you must always listen to them respectfully, for such is God's commandment in *Leviticus* XIX, where Our Lord God instructs us that *Coram cano capite consurge et honora personam senis* (19,32). And it means that you must rise to your feet when faced by an elder who approaches and is permitted to sit down, and you must always honour the person of an aged man. This, however, takes place when the elderly person is learned, respectable, careful of his honour, God-fearing, and of good moral character. For, if he were a mad old man with little moral sense, one ought not listen to him in such a manner; rather, one should avoid him like the devil. For sooner would a wicked old man corrupt a great multitude, if people were to listen or give credit to him, than would many young people together, for little credit is usually given to the young because they do not govern themselves wisely or virtuously. [...]

The sixth point is that one must listen to all kinds of words that are spoken well. And Seneca says, therefore, that one should not be drawn primarily by the authority and rank of the person who speaks, but should observe what he says; and, whoever he may be, if he speaks well and of things worth listening to, he should be heard. And he said, therefore, in another place that *Prudentis est officium non loquentem, sed quid loquitur attendere.* And he means that it is the duty of the wise man not to pay attention to the person who is speaking above all else, but rather, first and foremost, to observe, consider and think over what it is he is saying. And when Hugh, therefore, wished to show in his *Didascalicon*[4] how man should learn, he issued three pieces of advice. The first is that one should not disdain any piece of writing, for, at times, good things can be found in wicked books, just as roses can be found among thorns. The second is that, if there is something to be gained, you should not disdain other people, for humility is the portal to knowledge. The third is that

---

3   The text of the Latin Vulgate reads "...in medio *sermonum* ne adicias loqui" (emphasis added).*

4   *Didascalicon* III, 13.

you should never be ashamed to learn from anyone who wishes or is able to teach you, though he might be young, a layman, a foreigner or whoever it might be. And, speaking in favour of this very doctrine, Saint Augustine says that there is no man in the world who might be capable of teaching him from whom he should be ashamed to learn or whose teachings he should reject, having considered how great is the dignity of knowledge. The portal to this knowledge is called humility, which humility a man displays when he willingly humbles himself before another who is of a lower station than he, by confessing himself to be ignorant and that other more knowledgeable.

TC 961-964

2. REGARDING ONE'S TEACHER

2.1. *What type of men the sons of sovereigns should have as their teachers*

Moreover, according to what Alfarabius says in the said *Doctrinal*,[5] the teacher of sovereign's sons must be someone who is well-acquainted with and understands what he is teaching, is able to explain it well and has a fine and clear expository style, and who notices the qualities of his pupils and sets them to work upon the branch of knowledge towards which he sees that they are most inclined, for from such subjects will they draw greater benefit than from others. And, if he sees that they are coarse and dull-witted, he teaches them, at the very least, to maintain a sensible silence in the company of others, and sagely to remain there, using controlled and prudent gestures which do not display vulgarity to others, but rather cover it as much as possible, and he teaches them to reply briefly to each person in order to conceal any coarseness. And in order that they might not be known to be coarse in this way, they defer all important affairs until they have had private meetings which they set in motion or have others do so in order not to keep people waiting too long.

And this writer advises, above all, that the teachers of sovereign's sons should be honourable and well brought up and of good conscience. And he recommends this so that the said sons might not be

---

5 Cat. *Doctrinari or doctrinal*: a book studied in medieval schools and serving to broaden and complete customary grammatical teachings.*

set any bad examples by them nor adopt any evil vices from them. And he says that such teachers must prevent the sons of sovereigns from speaking about vile carnal acts at all costs, for speaking in this way makes them recall and desire women and, subsequently, it makes them sin with them. They must likewise deter them from uttering falsehoods for, according to the philosophers, this vice has great power over young men, and once they are accustomed to doing it, they cannot be reformed of it; and it is one of the foulest things in this world that, subsequently, when they occupy the position of lord, they should utter or commit or consent to falsehoods. They must also make sure that they train them to speak but little, and they must do this so that they do not speak deceitfully, for he who talks a great deal lies a great deal, and likewise so that they do not make stupid remarks, for young people are not very sensible and are overly eager, as a result of which, if they are too garrulous, they will necessarily make mistakes and will tell many lies. For this reason, this Doctor says, one must train them to deliberate before they speak in order that they grow accustomed to doing so and do not frequently have to take back what they have said when they have to govern.

Furthermore, he says that they must prevent them from conversing a great deal with women, from going to see them and from keeping paintings in which foul acts are portrayed, for, as their natures are already inclined towards evil, if the said things are added subsequently, they will quickly succumb to sin. They must teach them moreover to move their eyes discreetly and with maturity and good sense, and not to let their gaze dart about this way and that with their eyes wide open and their mouths gaping, for then it is clear that they are astounded by everything and such a manner of gazing reveals that they are fearful, stupid and lacking in good sense.

DC 556

2.2. *To whom in particular one cannot be sufficiently grateful, and how ingratitude was severely punished by the ancients*

Aristotle in the ninth book of his *Ethics* specified that there are three things to which man owes the greatest obligation and to which he must be more grateful than any others, and that to act reprehensibly towards these reveals the greatest possible lack of respect. For he says that *Diis, magistris et parentibus non potest equivalens reddi.*[6] And he means that nobody can either return, perform or grant to God, to the masters who have taught us or to our parents the degree of favour he has received from them. And without a shadow of doubt, nobody can do that which he is obliged to do with respect to God, for, as Saint Bernard says, justice, imprinted as this is by God upon our natures, proclaims that man owes his very being to the one who has created him. And as the poet said, regarding our teachers, one of the keys to learning is being able to honour one's own teachers, for by their instruction they adorn our souls with the very benefits we enjoy. Nature reveals this with respect to our parents likewise, for, since we have our being from them after God, it follows that we owe singular and particular reverence, respect and love to them after God.

TC 501

3. TEACHING AND THE SPOKEN WORD

In praise of speech

Besides, one must always be minded and willing to listen to good things from wherever they come, for man's sense of hearing enables him to learn many things, whence experience shows that one is much better acquainted with what one has learnt by listening and as a result of a person's oral explanations than what one has read or studied by oneself. And Saint Jerome says this in the third chapter of his prologue to the *Bible*, where he states that *Habet nescio quid latentis energiae vivae vocis actus et in aures discipuli de auctoris ore transfusa fortius sonat.*[7] And he thus means that the spoken word which issues from the mouth of the person who gives good instruction to others possesses within itself a hidden virtue, which is such that, as it reaches the ears of the person who hears it, it penetrates man's mind more forecefully and educates him better than any other thing. And, therefore, that great philosopher Socrates always encouraged men to listen a great deal and to speak but little. And he said that, for this reason, nature had given man two ears and only a single mouth, and also in order that

[6] Cf. note 1.
[7] *Epistle* 53.

wise men might learn about those things on which they would never
have passed judgement or sentence unless they had first been
informed by both sides.

TC 964

4. Education and playfulness

4.1. *The use of games as a pedagogical method*

And, therefore, you should know that Saint Augustine says in this particular respect that holy men at times play with their wives, but they
do so with the greatest caution, that is to say, by making concessions
to feminine fragility, which, generally speaking, has to be supported
in this way during the present life. However, they take care not to
undermine their commitment on this account to things which relate
to God, nor for any reason would they do such things other than with
women who were their wives. And, therefore, nobody should think of
taking amiss what that holy man Isaac did, in that case, when playing
with his spouse,[8] as certain inhuman men have done who, not only in
this respect, but also, if they see any man of note letting out a few
laughs or playing with small children, immediately begin to mutter
about it, saying that they are mad. And by such mutterings they reveal
that they do not recall that they were once young and were raised in
the midst of similar things, by which fact they display at the same time
great ingratitude towards those who raised them, whom they dishonour by such mutterings, hasty judgements and great inhumanity
towards children, who need to be raised in this manner amidst
caresses and games.

TC 536

4.2. *The need for leisure*

Which states particular recommendations regarding one's way of life

The second recommendation of the said philosopher with regard to
the sons of sovereigns was that they should devote themselves, after
their studies and other labours, to certain chaste delights and amuse-

---

[8] Cf. Gen 26,7-10.

ments, and this was because, according to what Aristotle demonstrates *in septimo Politicorum,*[9] if man were to apply himself intensely to work, his body could not endure this for long unless he interspersed it with certain delights. Cato, therefore, said: *Interpone tuis interdum gaudia curis.*[10] And he means this, namely that, if you wish to prolong your life then, at times, you must know how to intersperse your labours with certain permissible delights and pleasures. Man's strength, which lies within, acts upon his body as if this were its tool; and, thus, since no worker can labour effectively if the tool with which he labours is not in full working order, thus man can never do anything well unless his body is in full working order. And since, for one's body to enjoy such prime condition it helps a great deal to have some pleasure and relaxation, it is, therefore, fitting that, after he has laboured, man should have certain permissible pleasures. For this reason, Aristotle states *in octavo Politicorum* that permissible delights were, therefore, necessary in particular after one had ceased working, in order that a man who had nothing chaste to entertain him while resting, might not occupy his mind with improper deeds.

DC 557

4.3. *Which amusements are suitable for sovereigns and their grown-up sons*

In this particular respect, Andronicus teaches us which amusements are suitable for sovereigns and their grown-up sons, and he states the following rules first of all with regard to these. The first rule is that every worthy amusement must be honourable and pleasing to all. Insofar as he says that it must be honourable, they must take flight from and avoid foul, carnal entertainments, whether in vile deeds or foul language. It is a hideous blight and an abomination in a sovereign, he says, and it will lead him to be considered as vile and unworthy of any honour if, each time he seeks diversion, he seeks it with his wife; and it is even worse if he continually seeks relief in the company of another woman, for it reveals that he is a lecherous and womanising man who has lost his reason and all sense of shame.

For this reason Eliol, sovereign of Pamphilia, killed his king with the agreement of the entire kingdom, for, as a rule, he never took

---

9 The allusion matches more closely *Politics* VIII, 2-3. These chapters also underlie the later reference to "Aristotle *in octavo Politicorum*".

10 Cf. *Disticha Catonis* 3, 6.

relaxation in the company of his knights nor with his people, but rather in the company of his wife and his maidservants in his bedroom, according to what is stated in the *History of the East*. Similarly, noble sovereigns and noblemen must avoid ever listening to foul language or carnal filth from the lips of anyone while they are at their ease or laughing, and they must do so in order to preserve their purity as if it were a special pearl adorning the dignity of a sovereign. He says, moreover, that the amusements of a sovereign must be pleasing to all, for he who entertains the lord must not pass wind from above or below, nor indulge in hideous vulgarity, both of which arouse people to nausea and cause them great disgust, in the manner of things which are loathsome to everybody. For this reason, it is clear that if the entertainments of whoever wishes to amuse are worthy, he must take great care not to say or to do anything which might displease another. And certain minstrels who can never tell a joke without offending some other person present or speaking ill about someone who is absent do the opposite of this, and by such means they pollute their entertainment. And frequently have many minstrels lost their lives in this manner, though, let us hope, not their souls!

The second rule of the said philosopher was that great lords who wish to encounter ready diversion, can find it by strolling through pleasant open spaces; or by looking at broad expanses of land or sea; or by riding through green and beautiful places, full of trees, fish and other delightful things; or by riding through cities and towns at their leisure. Secondly, they can take pleasure at home in practising their fencing, which is a good skill for them to learn, or by devoting themselves to jumping or to throwing iron bars or stones, or by practising with the crossbow, which must be done in a private place with which they are familiar. Thirdly, they can listen to musical instruments or sing or have fine singers perform in their presence, accompanied by organs or other instruments or even unaccompanied. Fourthly, by going to hunt or fish, although hunting is the province rather of sovereigns; yet not all types of hunting become them, but only those which are respectable, such as hunting deer, lions, bears or boar and only when they are properly accompanied and never in any danger. Fifthly, playing chess or backgammon, but only for amusement, and on no account should they play dice or any game which excites them; playing cards does not behove them, as it is a game for women. Sixthly, in order to have recreation, they can listen to fine jesters and entertainers who know their profession well and are able to tell skilful jokes which are brief and do not cause offence to any other people, for, as Baldwin, the celebrated court jester of the king of France, once said, great wisdom is needed to play the fool properly in the presence of great lords. Seventhly, they can watch conjurors[11] and men who, without sinning, are able to perform conjuring tricks or who can jump or perform nimble movements with their bodies; and, although these things are forbidden by the Holy Church to bishops and prelates, they are not, however, to laymen, so long as the conjuror does not commit a sin, in anything he might do, by carrying out some superstitious rite of the devil according to some evil art. Eighthly, talking among agreeable companions about some pleasant topic, such as military or scholarly matters or something respectable, or joking with others and laughing and rejoicing decorously, without any excess or impropriety. This writer advises, however, that if the sovereign wishes to devote himself to laughing and to joking, he should not do so publicly out of consideration for his dignity since, as a rule, when somebody laughs he lacks composure and, as a result, this renders him dissolute, contemptible and worthy of scorn in the eyes of others, and this is something that every good sovereign must avoid at all costs. Ninthly, taking a journey through a city or close to a lake or through the countryside or along a river or by the sea, and by riding and broadening one's horizons. Tenthly, reading pleasant things about decent and beautiful subjects. Eleventhly, speaking with people they love and from whose presence they derive great solace or pleasure, whether this be their wife, their children, or some friend or particular servant of theirs whose conversation is agreeable, so that they might speak confidentially with them about matters which are familiar to them. Twelfthly, listening to items of news and having people who are readily able to discover them, and sovereigns can listen to such men at their leisure without having to believe what they say, for such men are usually great liars. Thirteenthly, smelling or washing one's hands, feet and face in fragrant waters, or thinking of pleasant, profitable and decent things.

And by such means can sovereigns readily find great amusement, should they require it, far from their bed, their meal table and their private apartments, according to the said philosopher.

DC 558

[11] Cat. *tragitador*. This term can also mean (court) acrobats or tumblers. Here it seems to refer to conjurors.*

5. DIET AND HOW TO LIVE

5.1. *Against excess of study*

Chapter CLXI, which states the ninth condition of a worthy pursuit

The ninth condition which every worthy pursuit must satisfy is that it be undertaken in moderation. And first of all, in this respect, you must note the following teaching, namely that one must not devote oneself to any pursuit to such an extent that one is completely incapable of doing anything else. And the reason is that such a pursuit is highly injudicious, regarding which Saint Jerome says that it shows that the person who undertakes it does not know how to offer it to God, since that person has not been able to add salt to it, that is to say, wisdom and discretion, for Our Lord God accepts the service of no one but that person who serves Him in a manner conforming to reason. And those who fast so much that, later on, they are unable to pray to God or to perform any other act of labour go against this teaching. And those who study so much that, subsequently, they have no time to pray, likewise, go against this same teaching, as do those who are so contemplative that, thereafter, they have no time to preach or to perform any work of piety. And, in general, all those who devote themselves and attend to worthy things so much that they are unable to do something else towards which they have an obligation, sin against this teaching.

In the fourth book of his *Didascalicon*, that great Doctor, Hugh, speaks about this manner of applying oneself, in the chapter where he states that one must not consent to reading too much, since it hinders contemplation, which is the soul's mirror and the life of the spirit. And, in this regard, he recounts that when a Holy man did the contrary, overcome and drawn as he was by the great joy he found in reading Holy Scripture, he arrived at such a state that he understood so much about his ill-considered studies, that it kept him from prayer and contemplation as well as from his other necessary works, until it was revealed to him through divine revelation that his studies were not pleasing to God nor beneficial to himself on account of their lack of prudence. Doctors say that apoplexy is a fatal illness, yet it is caused by a superfluity of beneficial humours; we note, likewise, that a lamp which is too full of oil extinguishes its flame, and thus a pursuit – whatever it may be, and however worthy it is in itself – which is not prudently undertaken causes more harm than it is worth and should rather be called a worldly affair than a spiritual labour.

SC 161

5.2. *How to lead an ideal life*

A chapter which states the ninth remedy against the sin of gluttony

The ninth remedy against the sin of gluttony is to study and consider with great diligence how one can protect oneself against this sin which is so deceptively bound up with need, for which reason, as Saint Bernard says, one cannot acquire this need without first passing through unruly sensual pleasures or delights in some shape or form, as has already been stated above.

And you should know that a monk that I have seen in this kingdom of ours, desiring to abstain from and repudiate the vile sin of gluttony, decided to do the following, namely, first of all, he ate alone and tried to consider without pause by what means and by how much he could decrease his gluttony without his having to suffer too greatly or to grow too weak. And, first, he forsook all banqueting and costly meats, such as fowl, the very best fish[12] and sauces, and all expensive wines and exquisite breads and he wished to eat only inexpensive foods. Furthermore, he reduced the quantity, for if he ate meat cooked on the spit he would not eat meat cooked in the pot as well or, if he had one fish, he would not eat another. And thus he ordered his servant not even to mention these things to him. Likewise, he abstained from every type of fruit there was, apart from that which he was bound to eat for the requirements of his health, such as raisins or medicinal fruits.[13] Similarly, he denied himself all sweetmeats made with honey or sugar, all kinds of milk as well as clarified butter and cheese, and also all sweet juices, such as those made from oranges,

[12] 'Fowl' (Cat. *carn de ploma*) here includes feathered birds or animals such as partridges, chickens, ducks, pigeons, etc. The 'very best fish' (Cat. *peix de tall*) here refers to large, hard-skinned fish; this was the most highly-prized kind of fish, in gastronomical terms, and was, therefore, the most expensive.

[13] According to medieval medicine, the excessive consumption of fruit led to an excess of phlegm, this being the source of a variety of illnesses. However, it was believed that fruit, when eaten in moderation, could have positive effects upon one's health. Raisins, for example, were recommended in the cure of illnesses relating to the chest and lungs. Arnald of Villanova recommended them as a laxative.

lemons and the like. In addition, he renounced all man-made confec-
tionery, such as nougat, doughnuts, spiced wine, wafer rolls and all
white wine and honey. Moreover, he forwent all varieties of stew, but
for the sake of his own sustenance alone would he eat a single one,
with the result that his entire diet consisted of bread and cheap wine
and of uncostly meats and fish, and little of each. He would eat ade-
quately at lunch and would have a very light dinner, and he would
accept his supper in order that he might be able to endure the night's
labours and so that he might sleep better and that he should awaken
earlier and be able to rise more cheerfully in order to meditate and to
say the divine offices, and this was necessary for him because he was
elderly. And he fulfilled his resolution to deprive himself out of love
for God so strictly and prudently that on no account would he do the
opposite, unless he were obliged to do so from obedience and, in such
a case, he would avoid all superfluity. He showed such moderation in
his drinking, that at lunch he would drink three suitably-sized cupfuls
of heavily diluted wine and at dinner he drank two of them and ate the
half of his meal consisting of bread and two eggs or the equivalent.

He never slept during the day, other than from the middle of May
to the middle of August or until the end of the said month.[14] He never
settled down in bed unless he had a great urge to sleep. He always rose
as soon as he had awoken and began to say his prayers. He always
spoke in Latin in order to become more conversant with it, to teach it
to others and to cause those with whom he was talking to speak it, and
he did not speak at length but only for as long as was permissible in
and allowed by his order. Never at night would he leave his cell nor
permit anyone else to come to his. He avoided women and laypeople
like the devil. He never slept at the dawn hour, but devoted that time
to contemplation. He divided up his entire life between saying his
offices, seeing to the needs of his body, offering prayers or formulat-
ing something in his studies for the sake of the salvation of the people.
He did not have any more clothes than those he absolutely needed
nor did he ever amass money or any worldly goods. And this moderation in his way of life was endorsed by many holy people. He never
wished for anything special nor accepted it willingly, though, if he

[14] Medieval medicine considered the practice of taking afternoon naps highly
harmful. However, the majority of religious orders allowed it during the hottest days of
summer.

accepted anything, he would give it to his community or to some other party who had need of it. He always obeyed his community and made efforts to observe the rites of his order.

TC 402

5.3. *On how keeping fast elevates the understanding*

The fourth benefit that keeping fast offers is that it ensures that man's understanding is uplifted, elevated and prepared for wisdom and knowledge as well as for the profound consideration and contemplation of lofty, heavenly matters. And, therefore, the holy prophets were all greatly given to fasting, as we read of Elijah in particular, to whom a raven brought food each day (3 Kings 17,6). Likewise, that holy prophet Daniel who did not wish, either he or his companions, to eat or drink the rich food or the wine from the table of the king of Babylon, but instead ate vegetables and drank water (Dan 1,8-16). We read, therefore, at the beginning of the Book of Daniel that Our Lord God gave them more good sense, wisdom and learning than all the lettered men and philosophers there were in the empire of Chaldea (Dan 1,17). [...] And, likewise, the holy apostles, before they had received the Holy Spirit and its gifts of wisdom and knowledge, and of speaking all tongues and other gifts besides, first of all abstained from food for ten days while they said prayers, as is shown *in Actibus Apostolorum* (1,12-26).

Likewise, through fasting the saintly hermits and monks of old arrived at such a lofty knowledge of divine matters that never has a philosopher or great scholar been able to rival it. Follow the example set by that glorious and noble Saint Anthony, who was always fasting in the desert and whom heathen philosophers came to visit in order to ask him for arguments by which he might demonstrate the Christian faith to them, which he did most nobly. And when they realised that he was completely unlettered, they asked him how he knew so much without any learning.

And he posed the following question to them, saying:

"Tell me what came first, wisdom or learning?"

And when they said that wisdom came first, he replied:

"So, you should not be astonished that God in his mercy has given me wisdom without learning, given that I am here in this place of deserts, performing penance and fasting without pause out of love for Him."

Likewise, Saint Benedict, who spent so long fasting in the desert, was worthy of overcoming terrible temptations of the flesh; and, besides this, before he died, he saw the entire world in a single point all at once, as a result of which some people suppose that, in the New Testament, he had received a special dispensation to perceive the divine essence. Likewise, Saint Benedict says that while he was praying and fasting under some beech trees, the *Bible* was revealed and fully explained to him. And the holy prophets of the Old Testament, despite the fact they spoke in the most elevated language, included many among them who were coarse peasants in terms of their accomplishments and their natures, such as Jeremiah, Amos and Jonah and others who, by fasting and prayer, rose to the lofty intelligence pertaining to prophets. Solomon said, therefore, *Ecclesiastes* II: "I resolved in my heart to abstain from wine, that I might be more disposed to learn wisdom" (2,3).

Similarly, when the philosophers of old themselves wished to contemplate lofty things, they would climb through the mountains and deserts, and while fasting in these places and leading very harsh lives, they rose to a very great intelligence, as we read of Parmenides, who spent fifteen years studying geometry high upon a rocky crag in Egypt. Similarly, we note from experience that children learn more in the morning before they have eaten than after they have had lunch. And we note the same thing in ourselves. For this reason, it is clear that fasting is the mother of intelligence, wisdom and knowledge.

TC 320

5.4. A full and fat stomach does not permit a man's mind to be sharp

The second main reason why men must greatly avoid the sin of gluttony is out of love for man himself, for great are the ills which gluttony causes in men, both with respect to the soul and the body. And, first of all, this vice harms man with regard to his soul, for it renders it dull-witted, depriving it of any good sense. Saint Jerome says, therefore, that *Nichil adeo obruit intelligentiam ut comessatio et ebrietas*. And he means that there is nothing which does away with man's understanding so greatly as eating and drinking too much. And we can see this from experience at all times, for a man who eats too much can hardly maintain control over his body. And similarly, his stomach never ceases to send vapours to his head which affect his brain; it also exhausts his natural faculties and completely confounds them so that he does not know what he is doing.

And, for this reason, the lifespan of a glutton is greatly reduced, for you should know for sure that eating little and in moderation greatly prolongs one's life, and eating beyond one's needs causes large fistulae to form, and often leads to illnesses and ulcers, as a result of which it is fitting that the life of a man be shortened. And, if eating causes harm such as this, excessive drinking causes worse, for the mind of a heavy drinker is almost never clear, and he is close to being an idiot, as we are bound to mention below when we speak of the sin of drunkenness. And, for this reason, Saint Jerome said *quod venter pinguis non genuit tenuem sensum.*[15] And he means that a full and fat stomach does not permit a man's mind to be sharp. And those who are in the habit of studying the sciences can confirm this by experience, for nobody can arrive with perspicacity at any serious conclusion when his stomach is full; whence, although after having had lunch one can debate competently regarding what one has seen and read earlier, nobody, however, who knows anything about studying will ever study at such a time, for one's understanding is clouded by the vapours which rise from one's stomach to one's head. And besides, in that case, if he were to begin studying, a man would be overcome by the urge to sleep, and his stomach would rupture itself through his leaning over, and as a result he would be at risk of dying. For, under such circumstances, the food would be packed tight in his stomach and would form a stone and would not be able to be digested, but rather would remain there as solid as a rock and would upset his stomach and cause him indigestion. And, likewise, this type of study greatly damages one's eyes for, in such a case, nature, wishing to assist the part which is at work, namely the eyes, sends all the vapours which issue from the stomach there and, as a consequence, this form of studying is the means by which a man who studies under such conditions gradually develops cataracts in his eyes and thus, in time, loses his sight.

And as a result of these things the main theme becomes clear, namely that a full stomach upsets and impedes one's understanding, besides the other afore-mentioned ills which it causes to man. And on account of these things, Seneca said that a gluttonous man should live among the brute animals and was deemed to be brutish, given that he had forfeited his understanding through gluttony and, despite all that, still wished to gluttonise.

TC 301

[15] Epistle 52 (*Ad Nepotianum*).

5.5. *On how and why fat people are, at times, learned and knowledgeable*

Somebody may say in this regard that there are many knowledgeable and learned people who are fat and fleshy, and that, when they have eaten more heartily and drunk more deeply, they are better disposed to conducting fuller debate and to discussing scholarly affairs and matters requiring great acuity. To this I answer by means of three points. The first is that I do not wish to imply by anything that I have said, that Our Lord, who fulfils the desires of both the wicked and the good in abundance, does not, at times, give knowledge and natural good judgement to men who are fat or who are averse to fasting.

The second point is that, at times, such plentiful, scholarly talk and discussion after eating and drinking is due to the warming that takes place in man, which causes him to speak about what he already knows. However, that particular time is not suitable for innovative thoughts about anything which is lofty or difficult, on account of the vapours which rise from the opening of the stomach to the brain. It is true that fat men have much phlegm in their brains – and on account of this, as a rule, they always snore when they are sleeping – and for this very reason the vapours from their stomachs which rise to their heads find greater impediment in them than they do in men who are dry and slender, to the heads of whom these vapours rise swiftly. And this may be the reason why, after lunch, fat men are able to debate more effectively than slim ones, except when slender people, immediately after they have eaten, consume sugared almonds or apples or something which hinders the rise of such vapours.

The third point is that such debating and garrulousness in fat people after lunch is not a case of their acquiring or seeking knowledge; rather, it is a case of their implementing and speaking about things that they have already learnt. And from this it is clear that what they eat or drink does not assist them in their knowledge, even though it inflames them to talk about what they have learnt and, in fact, already know.

And from this it follows that anything which I have said in contrary to the above does not contradict the principal theme, namely that fasting greatly clarifies man's understanding and disposes him towards learning, while gluttony and excessive eating are a severe impediment to knowledge, according to what is said by Seneca. And Saint Jerome states that nothing coarsens the understanding as much as excessive eating and drinking. And this is stated by Scripture as well, *Sapientiae*

IX, which says that *Corpus quod corrumpitur aggravat animam et terrena habitatio deprimit sensum intus inhabitantem* (9,15). And it means that our bodies, which continually waste away and return to the soil, weigh down our souls heavily, and do not permit these latter to raise their thoughts towards the lofty things which they are naturally inclined and disposed to consider; and the earthly habitation, that is to say, the body itself, insofar as it consists of earth and weighty stuff, weakens and coarsens the judgement of our intellect, which becomes unable to perceive almost anything with acuity; abstinence from food, however, is of assistance to it to the extent that, when one's body is less strong and less laden with flesh, with blood and with food, it is all the more disposed to having profound thoughts regarding heavenly matters.

TC 321